haiku knits

haiku knits

25 SERENELY BEAUTIFUL PATTERNS
INSPIRED BY JAPANESE DESIGN

TANYA ALPERT

Foreword by Erika Knight

WATSON-GUPTILL PUBLICATIONS / NEW YORK

First published in 2009 by Watson-Guptill Publications,
an imprint of the Crown Publishing Group,
a division of Random House, Inc., New York
www.crownpublishing.com
www.watsonguptill.com

Library of Congress Control Number: 2009922078

ISBN: 978-0-8230-9807-1

Printed in China

2 3 4 5 6 7 8 9 / 17 16 15 14 13 12 11 10

Designer: Vera Fong

To my daughters, Naomi and Dena, and my husband Leon,

who inspired, encouraged, and supported me every step of the way.

To the loving memory of my mother and my father,

who said that the luckiest person is the one who manages to accomplish

three things in life: plant a tree, raise a child, and write a book.

acknowledgments

There are many people I would like to thank for support and faith in this project. Professional collaboration and friendship with these wonderful people means a great deal to me.

I would like to thank my editors, *Joy Aquilino* and *Linda Hetzer*, for the care with which they reviewed the original manuscript; their direction, assistance, and guidance have been invaluable to me.

I am also grateful to my agent, *Joy Tutela*, for standing by me all the way through.

Thanks are also due to a talented photographer, *Michael Turek*, for taking wonderful photos of my designs, which made this book beautiful.

I am grateful to my dearest friend, *Anabel Mintz*, for believing in me, encouraging me, and giving me inspiration to create some of my designs; and my close friend, *Diane Drake*, for helping and supporting me along the way.

Special thanks and gratitude are given to members of my Knitting Club, and especially *Terri Pavelko, Sharon Wylie, Valerie Ellison, Melinda Woodstra, Helen Haskell, Cathy Hays, Greet Hostetler, Jeanne Olson, Linda Johnson, Sandi Brown, Ann Marie Ebeling, Geraldine Minott*, and *Elonne Petrin* for their great ideas, suggestions, encouragement, and support.

I also wish to acknowledge *Nancy Muschek* and *Aphrodite Sacorafas* for their invaluable help.

Many thanks to our good friends *Jay* and *Razia Richter* for encouraging me to open my knitting boutique, which in turn led to creating this book.

I am grateful to my family, my brother *Peter* and my uncle *Boris*, who believed in me, and especially to my daughters, *Naomi* and *Dena*, who encouraged and supported me, and gave me ideas and inspirations.

And of course, it was my husband, *Leon*, who provided me with vital encouragement and support during many months of hard work: thanks to him for this and many other things.

foreword

In *Haiku Knits*, knitwear designer Tanya Alpert shares her innate sensibilities, influenced by haiku poetry and the natural world, through a unique collection of knitted designs that is modern, simple, and very wearable.

I share this ethos of a pared-down simplicity with Tanya. If all creativity springs from nature—as I believe it does—then the pieces she has created are wind, water, snow, and light knitted into effortless beauty.

From the innovation of "Chrysanthemum," a cardigan based on a Japanese kimono, to the gossamer-fineness of "Hazy Moon," a whisper-light scarf, Tanya's designs go beyond the traditional. The trick lies in giving old material a new twist. Among my personal favorites is "Evening Mist," a deceptively unelaborate evening chemise, using wool–stainless steel yarn to achieve a sculptural silhouette.

Because one cannot spin wind and light into garments and accesseries without guidance, Tanya's clear, concise patterns and detailed schematics aid the knitting experience, and her invaluable "how-to" techniques are a reassuring accompaniment.

Michael Turek's perceptive photography harmonizes with Tanya's designs, making this a book that you will want to possess and peruse endlessly, and Tanya's insightful comments allow a glimpse into a personal journey that will inspire you to travel with her!

Erika Knight

contents

preface

I was born in Kiev, Ukraine, in 1961, and designing has been my passion since childhood. Starting with doll clothes, then making clothes for myself and my family and creating gifts for friends, I've done it all, and most of it out of necessity. Fortunately, I loved it. Throughout my childhood I helped my family by knitting warm sweaters for cold winters, because decent clothes, like food, were scarce. The idea that someday I would open my own knitting boutique wasn't even a dream at that point.

In 1982, I graduated with honors from the Art College in Kiev, Ukraine with a degree in product design, and four of my art pieces were chosen for the college museum. After graduating, starting a family, and then moving to the United States in 1988, I had no idea what the future would hold, but I knew I would always have to be connected to art. Whether working as a graphic designer or creating fiber art pieces, designing jewelry or knitwear pieces, this one aspect of my life had to remain constant.

In 1995, working as a graphic artist, I also started creating fiber art pieces and was invited to join the Pacific Quilt Artists group. One of my pieces was shown at California Design 2000 in San Francisco, and then another one at Craft USA 2002 in New York, where my work was one of only eighty-six pieces accepted from across the county. I knew then I had a passion for fiber. My work has been shown in art galleries, and featured in magazines. I was commissioned by the Susan Street Gallery in Solana Beach to design a fiber art piece for the new Kaiser Permanente Hospital facility in National City, California.

Three years ago, my love of knitting and my desire to share this passion inspired me to open Knitting by the Beach. I wanted to create an environment where people could come together to explore and share in one another's creativity, and to enjoy the therapeutic aspects of knitting. As my clientele grew and I began to get to know my customers more personally, I realized that designing for them was my calling. Many of these women have discriminating taste and a distinctive, sophisticated style. Creating wearable designs that would appeal to them became my goal.

I was especially intrigued by Japanese yarns with their unique textures and understated beauty. I began mixing them with more traditional yarns to create new designs, while incorporating some of the elements of Japanese aesthetics. Two of the main tenets of Japanese aesthetics are economy in the use of space and materials, and asymmetry. As in a haiku, in the expression of emotion and thought, an economical use of space and time seems especially appropriate today. As for asymmetry, it suggests fluidity and motion. Bridging elements of Japanese aesthetics with our Western fashion was very exciting to me and became the genesis for *Haiku Knits*.

The combination of different textures, twisted cables, decorative seams, and asymmetric shapes, was inspired by traditional *wabi* (beauty that is incomplete) and *sabi* (beauty that comes with age), where imperfections are celebrated. The shape of each design brings the Japanese reverence for fabric to the Western ideal of clothes that are cut and shaped to the body: They focus on the coexistence of the knitted fabric and the body. Feminine without being frilly and minimalist without being severe, these patterns are perfectly suited to our modern lifestyle. The twenty-five designs featured in *Haiku Knits* celebrate originality, simplicity, sophisticated color, and comfortable fit.

Tanya

lingering snow

Soft winter wrap

Yochino cherry petals

Caress the waiting earth

snowflake *lacy long-sleeve cozy*

This beautiful wrap, created from one long rectangle with openings for the sleeves, is knit with two strands of yarn held together, a wool yarn and a mohair-silk blend. The rectangle has a panel of knitted lace along each side that adds a decorative note while also keeping the wrap lightweight. The sleeves are worked by picking up stitches around the armhole openings, then knitting in the round from the top down, decreasing as you knit until you form the cuffs.

MATERIALS

- Cascade 220 or Superwash 220 (4/medium weight; 100% Peruvian highland wool; 3½ oz/100g, 220 yds/201m): 5 (5, 6) skeins of Cascade #8505 or Superwash #817
- Rowan Kidsilk Spray (3/lightweight; 70% super kid mohair, 30% silk; 0.88 oz/25g, 229 yds/210m): 5 (5, 6) balls of Graphite #570
- One each of sizes 9 and 11 (5.5mm and 8mm) 16" and 24" long circular needles. *Adjust needle size if necessary to obtain gauge.*
- Stitch markers
- Decorative shawl pin, approx. 4–6" long

GAUGE (with both yarns held together)

14 sts and 18 rows = 4" in St st on larger needles

12 sts and 18 rows = 4" in Lace Patt on larger needles

18 sts and 22 rows = 4" in 2 x 2 Rib on smaller needles

To save time, take time to check gauge.

STITCH PATTERNS

Stockinette Stitch (St st)

Row 1 (RS): Knit across.

Row 2 (WS): Purl across.

Repeat Rows 1 and 2.

2 x 2 Rib Stitch (multiple of 4)

Row 1: *K2, p2; rep from *.

Repeat Row 1.

Lace Pattern (multiple of 2)

Row 1: *K2tog, yo; repeat from * to end.

Row 2: Purl.

Row 3: *Yo, k2tog; repeat from * to end.

Row 4: Purl.

Repeat Rows 1 through 4.

SKILL LEVEL

Easy

SIZE

One size fits most
(bust sizes from 34" to 42")

FINISHED MEASUREMENTS

Width of panel: 24"

Total length of rectangle: 61"

RIGHT FRONT

With larger needles and 1 strand of each yarn held
  together, CO 76 sts.

Row 1 (RS): K5, place marker (pm), [k2tog, yo] 10 times,
  pm, k26, pm [k2tog, yo] 10 times, pm, k5.

Row 2 (WS): Purl.

Row 3: K5, sl m, [yo, k2tog] 10 times, sl m, k26, sl m, [yo,
  k2tog] 10 times, sl m, k5.

Row 4: Purl.

Repeat these 4 rows until piece measures 14".

Divide for Right Armhole

Row 1 (RS): K5, [k2tog, yo] 10 times, k21. Attach a second
  set of yarns and BO 2 sts. Continue with the added
  yarn, k2, [k2tog, yo] 10 times, k5.

Row 2 (WS): Purl to the BO stitches; change yarns and P to
  end.

Row 3: K5, [yo, k2tog] 10 times, k21. Change yarns k3, [yo,
  k2tog] 10 times, k5.

Row 4: Purl as for Row 2.

Continue working both sides at the same time until armhole opening measures 9".

Join Armhole and Back

Row 1 (RS): K5, [k2tog, yo] 10 times, pm, k21, CO 2 sts,
  and using the same strand of yarn, k3, pm, [k2tog, yo]
  10 times, k5.

Row 2 (WS): Purl.

Row 3: K5, [yo, k2tog] 10 times, sl m, k26, sl m, [yo, k2tog]
  10 times, k5.

Row 4: Purl, cut second set of yarns, leaving a tail.

Resume working 4-row patt for 15".

Divide for Left Armhole

Repeat instructions for Divide for Right Armhole and Join
  Armhole and Back, above.

LEFT FRONT

Resume working 4-row patt for 14".

BO all sts.

SLEEVES

With larger 16" circular needle, pick up and loosely knit
  50 sts evenly around each sleeve opening, starting from
  the center, Point A, of the wider Stockinette panel. Place
  marker. Join and work in rounds, decreasing every 8th
  round 1 st before and 1 st after the marker 7 times.
  Change to smaller 16" circular needle and work in 2 x 2
  rib even for 8".

BO all sts.

FINISHING

Weave in all tails. Block lightly, folding under 2 sts of 5-st
  Stockinette border.

snowflake

lacy long-sleeve cozy

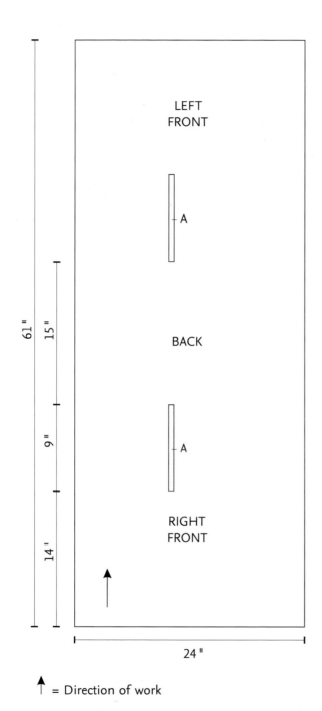

LEFT
FRONT

A

BACK

9"

A

RIGHT
FRONT

61"

15"

14"

24"

↑ = Direction of work

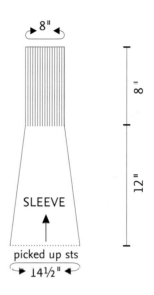

8"

8"

12"

SLEEVE

picked up sts

14½"

cocoon _twisted cable pullover_

This twisted cable _pullover reminds me of our lives: full of twists and turns, as we fall and rise, struggle and evolve, to finally emerge renewed and stronger. The yarn I used has a silky texture, subtle colors, and, for me, a sense of comfort, so I was inspired to create something familiar yet new, like an old cable with a new twist. To make this dramatic cable, you turn the knitting 180 degrees before you knit the stitches from the cable needle. Knit continuously in reverse stockinette stitch, the pullover has a classic fit with a funnel neck and elbow-length sleeves._

MATERIALS

- Rowan Cocoon (5/bulky weight; 80% merino wool, 20% kid mohair; 3½ oz/100g, 126 yds/115m): 5 (6, 7) balls of Craft #809
- One each of sizes 11 and 13 (8mm and 9mm) 24" long circular needles. _Adjust needle size if necessary to obtain the correct gauge._
- Large cable needle (cn)
- Stitch markers (m)
- Stitch holders
- Row counter
- Tapestry needle

GAUGE

14 sts and 16 rows = 4" in St st on size 11 (8mm) needle
To save time, take time to check gauge.

STITCH PATTERNS

Reverse Stockinette Stitch (rev St st)
Row 1 (RS): Purl across.
Row 2 (WS): Knit across.
Repeat Rows 1 and 2.

Stockinette Stitch (St st)
Row 1 (RS): Knit across.
Row 2 (WS): Purl across.
Repeat Rows 1 and 2.

Twisted Cable Pattern (over 20 sts)
Row 1 (RS): Place 10 sts on cn and hold in front of work, k10, twist 10 sts on cn 180 degrees to the left, k10 from cn.
Rows 2, 4, 6, 8, 10, 12, 14, 16, 18 (WS): P20.
Rows 3, 5, 7, 9, 11, 13, 15, 17 (RS): K20.

SKILL LEVEL

Intermediate

SIZES

Small (Medium, Large).
Instructions are for smallest size, with changes for other sizes noted in parentheses as necessary.

FINISHED MEASUREMENTS

Bust: 34 (36, 40)"
Length: 24½ (25½, 26½)"
Sleeve length: 11 (11, 11)"

Front Collar

Work 48 (52, 54) sts as established (knitting the K sts and purling the P sts). Place the rem 12 (15, 18) right shoulder sts on st holder. Turn and work the center 36 sts, placing the rem 12 (15, 18) left shoulder sts on another st holder. (Label the two st holders Right and Left.) Work the center 36 sts as established for 3". BO loosely.

BACK
Back Collar

CO 36 sts. Starting with a RS row: K20, p16 for 3½", ending with a WS row.

Underarm Shaping for the Armhole

Work Back Collar sts as above, then pick up and purl sts from the right shoulder st holder. Work right shoulder and Back Collar sts as established, then join the sts from the left shoulder st holder, 60 (66, 72) sts.

Begin working 18-row Twisted Cable Patt, starting with Row 1, for 8 (8½, 9)".

CO 3 sts at the beginning of next 2 rows, ending with 66 (72, 78) sts. Continue working in established patt for 17 (17½, 18)". BO loosely.

SLEEVES

With size 13 (9mm) needles and RS facing, pick up and knit 42 (44, 46) sts around armhole opening.

Work in St st, decreasing 1 st at each side every 10th row 3 times. Work until sleeve measures 11" or to desired length. Change to smaller needles and work in St st for 1".

BO all sts.

FINISHING

Block pieces lightly, avoiding cables. With wrong sides of Back and Front facing, sew side seams one stitch in from the edge to create a decorative seam on the outside of the garment. With RS facing, sew sleeves and collar seams with traditional mattress stitch.

FRONT

With smaller needles CO 66 (72, 78) sts.

Row 1 (WS): K1 (edge stitch), k30 (33, 36), pm, p20, pm, k14 (17, 20), k1 (edge stitch).

Row 2 (RS): K1 (edge stitch), p14 (17, 20), sl m, k20, sl m, p30 (33, 36), k1 (edge stitch).

Repeat Rows 1 and 2 for a total of 15 rows (approx 3½"), ending with a WS row.

Begin counting and work the 18-row Twisted Cable Pattern over the 20 sts between the markers. This 18-row repeat is continued throughout the construction of the garment. Work 17 (17½, 18)" from the CO edge, ending with a WS row.

Underarm Shaping for the Armhole

Bind off 3 sts at the beginning of the next 2 rows.

Continue working 60 (66, 72) sts even for 7½ (8, 8½)" for armhole.

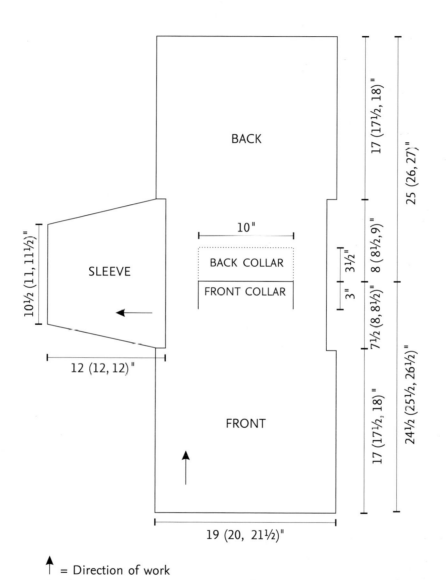

BACK

SLEEVE

10"

BACK COLLAR

FRONT COLLAR

FRONT

10½ (11, 11½)"

12 (12, 12)"

19 (20, 21½)"

17 (17½, 18)"

25 (26, 27)"

3" 3½"

8 (8½, 9)"

7½ (8, 8½)"

17 (17½, 18)"

24½ (25½, 26½)"

↑ = Direction of work

pagoda

tiered-loop hat and scarf

When my dear friend Anabel Mintz asked me to make an unusual hat with tiered loops, I immediately thought of pagodas. Those tiered towers with multiple eaves are beautiful places of worship designed to keep sacred relics safe. Since our heads are quite valuable to us I found this parallel to be amusing, and an inspiration to me to create the perfect marriage of beauty and function. This simple rolled-brim hat is quick to knit, and the bouclé yarn adds depth to the tiers of loops, making it both beautiful and fun to wear. The matching scarf is knit in two pieces and then joined in the center back.

MATERIALS

- RYC Cashsoft DK (3/light weight; 57% extra-fine merino, 33% acrylic microfiber, 10% cashmere; 1¾ oz/50g; 142 yds/130m): 3 balls of Black #519 (A) for the hat, and 3 balls of Black #519 (A) for the scarf
- Habu Textiles A-23 (3/light weight; 47% cotton, 38% silk, 13% twill woven; ½ oz/14g, 46 yds/42m): 3 balls of Black #10 (B) for the hat, and 3 balls of Black #10 (B) for the scarf
- *For the hat:* One each of size 9 (5.5mm) 16" long circular and double-pointed needles (dpn)
- *For the scarf:* Size 10 (6mm) needles
  Adjust needle size if necessary to obtain the correct gauge.
- Stitch markers (rn)
- One tapestry needle

GAUGE

For the hat: 14 sts and 24 rows = 4" with Yarn A doubled
For the scarf: 12 sts and 24 rows = 4" with Yarn A doubled
To save time, take time to check gauge.

STITCH PATTERNS

Stockinette Stitch (St st) *(for the hat when knit in the round)*
Round 1: Knit.
Repeat every round.

Stockinette Stitch (St st) *(for the scarf when knit flat)*
Row 1 (RS): Knit across
Row 2 (WS): Purl across.
Repeat Rows 1 and 2.

SKILL LEVEL

Easy

FINISHED MEASUREMENTS

Hat: Head circumference: 20–22"
Scarf: Finished rectangle: 6" x 56"

Loop Stitch Pattern

Knit 1 st, but do not slip it off the left needle. Bring the yarn to the front between the needles. Pass the yarn clockwise around your left thumb to form a 2½" loop. Return the yarn back between the needles and knit into the same knit st again, this time slipping it off the left needle.

Bring the yarn forward between the needles and wrap it over the right needle to make 1 st. Pass the 2 sts just worked over this stitch. Pull the loop on your thumb to tighten it, then slip the loop off your thumb.

PATTERN NOTE

This hat and scarf are knit with Yarn A doubled throughout. The loops are made with 3 strands: 1 of Yarn B and 2 of Yarn A.

HAT

With Yarn A doubled, CO 72 sts, place marker (pm), and join in a rnd, being careful not to twist the cast-on row. Knit 7 rnds.

Rnd 8 (and every following 8th round): Attach Yarn B to doubled Yarn A and work Loop Stitch Patt in every st of the rnd. Cut Yarn B, leaving a tail to weave in. Continue with Yarn A doubled for next 7 rnds. Work until hat measures 5½" from CO edge.

Crown Shaping

Continue with Loop Stitch Patt on every 8th rnd, then change to dpn, with sts evenly distributed, when crown becomes too tight for circular needle. Begin crown shaping:

Rnd 1: *K7, k2tog, pm; repeat from * to end of rnd. (Note: Place different color markers from the one indicating beginning of round).

Rnd 2: Knit.

Rnd 3: *K6, k2tog; repeat from * to end.

Rnd 4: Knit.

Rnd 5: *K5, k2tog, repeat from * to end.

Rnd 6: Knit.

Rnd 7: *K4, k2tog, repeat from * to end.

Rnd 8: Knit.

Rnd 9: *K3, k2tog, repeat from * to end.

Rnd 10: Knit.

Rnd 11: *K2, k2tog, repeat from * to end.

Rnd 12: Knit.

Rnd 13: *K1, K2tog, repeat from * to end.

Rnd 14: Knit.

Rnd 15: *K2tog, repeat from * to end.

Cut yarn, leaving 12" tail. Use tapestry needle to draw tail through rem sts. Pull up tight and fasten off to WS of hat. Weave in loose ends.

SCARF

Scarf Half (make 2)

With Yarn A doubled, CO on 20 sts. Work in St st for 6 rows, knitting first and last sts on every row. End with the WS row.

Row 7 (RS): Loop Stitch Patt.

Row 8 (WS): Knit.

Row 9 (RS): Knit.

Rows 10–12: Work in St st, knitting first and last sts on every row.

Repeat Rows 7–12 twice. Continue working in St st until piece measures 28" from CO edge. Place stitches on st holder.

FINISHING

Join 2 pieces in center back with Kitchener stitch. Weave in ends and steam gently on the wrong side.

fallen leaves *cabled wrap*

When leaves are falling *and winter is approaching, think of enveloping yourself in this beautiful cabled wrap made from a bulky-weight wool blend. The repeated vertical cables make a dramatic impact and, at the same time, flatter every body type. Worked in one long rectangular piece, this wrap is a great way to try your first cable project.*

MATERIALS

- Schoeller+Stahl Wonderwool (5/bulky weight; 51% virgin wool, 49% acrylic; 1¾ oz/50g; 93 yds/85m): 6 (7, 8) balls of Bordeaux #26
- One each of sizes 10 and 11 (6mm and 8mm) 29" long circular needles. *Adjust needle size if necessary to obtain gauge.*
- Stitch holders
- Stitch markers (m)
- Cable needle (cn)
- Decorative shawl pin, approx 4–6" long

GAUGE

18 sts and 20 rows = 4" in a pattern stitch on larger needles
To save time, take time to check gauge.

STITCH PATTERNS

2 x 2 Rib Stitch (even number of sts)
Row 1 (RS): K2, p2, repeat across.
Row 2 (WS): Knit the knit sts, purl the purl sts.
Repeat Rows 1 and 2.

Cable Pattern (multiple of 10 + 2)
Row 1 (Cable Row): P2, *C8B, p2, repeat from* to end.
Rows 2, 4, 6, and 8 (WS): K2, *p8, k2, repeat from* to end.
Rows 3, 5, and 7 (RS): P2, *k8, p2, repeat from* to end.
Repeat Rows 1–8.

Cable Stitch (C8B)
Sl 4 sts onto cn and hold in back, k4, then k4 from cn.

WRAP

Bottom Edge
With larger needles, CO 162 (182, 202) sts.
Rows 1,3, and 5 (RS): P2, *k8, p2, repeat from* to end.

SKILL LEVEL

Intermediate

SIZES

Small (Medium, Large).
Instructions are for smallest size, with changes for other sizes noted in parentheses as necessary.

FINISHED MEASUREMENTS

17 (18½, 20½)" x 40 (44½, 48½)"

Row 2, 4 (WS): K2, *p8, k2, repeat from* to end. Start Cable Patt, beginning with Row 6. Continue working in Cable Patt until piece measures 6½ (7, 8)".

Armhole Shaping

Note: End with Row 4 or 6 of Cable Patt (depending on the size) before starting Armhole Shaping.

Next Row (RS): Work 50 (60, 70) sts, Purl front and back (Pf&b) in the next P st. Place these 52 (62, 72) sts on st holder for Right Front.

Pf&b in next st, work foll 68 (78, 78) sts, then Pf&b in last st for Back. Place rem 41 (41, 51) sts on a second st holder to be used for Left Front.

Back

Continue working in established Cable Patt on Back until piece measures 6½ (7, 8)" from armhole opening. Place Back sts on st holder.

Right Front

Place Right Front sts on needles with WS facing. Attach yarn and work in established cable pattern until Right Front measures 6½ (7, 8)" from armhole opening. Place Right Front sts on st holder.

Left Front

With right side facing, attach yarn to armhole opening and inc (Pf&b) into 1st st, work rem 40 (40, 50) sts for total of 42 (42, 52) Continue in Cable Patt until piece measures 6½ (7, 8)" from armhole opening. End with RS row.

Join

Place Back and Right Front sts on needle with Left Front.

Next Row (WS): While continuing in Cable patt work Left Front stitches to the last knit st. K2tog with first knit st of Back; place marker (pm). Work Back stitches to last knit st, k2tog with first knit st of Right Front, pm, work to end. 164 (184, 204) sts.

Next Row (RS): Work Right Front to m and p2tog, work Back stitches to second m, p2tog, work rem Left Front sts. 162 (182, 202) sts.

Continue working in Cable Patt for 3 (3½, 3½)". End with the WS on Row 2 of Cable Patt.

Next Row (RS): K1, p1, *k2tog, k1, p2, repeat from* to end.

Next Row (WS): Work in 2 x 2 rib for 1". BO all sts.

Front Bands

With smaller needles and RS facing, pick up and knit 64 (72, 82) sts from Left Front side. Work in 2 x 2 rib for 2".

BO neatly.

Repeat for Right Front Band.

FINISHING

Use a decorative shawl pin as closure.

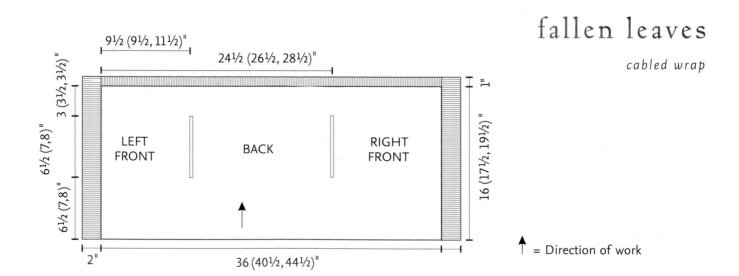

fallen leaves

cabled wrap

↑ = Direction of work

wind and stream

Sitting quietly

Near a window, silence . . .

Laconic beauty

chrysanthemum
kimono-style cardigan

Originally, kimono was simply the Japanese word for clothing, but today we use kimono to refer to the traditional dress of Japan. In the Heian period (794–1192), a new clothes-making technique was developed, known as the straight-line-cut method. This technique involved cutting pieces of fabric in straight lines and sewing them together. Straight-line-cut kimonos offered many advantages: They were flattering to all body shapes, easy to fold, and suitable for any weather. Even though the kimono has changed over time, its simple shape has remained the same. This simplicity inspired me to create a straight-line kimono sweater named for the official flower of Japan.

MATERIALS

- Sublime Cashmere Merino Silk Aran (4/medium weight; 75% Extra Fine Merino, 20% Silk, 5% Cashmere; 1¾ oz/50g, 94 yds/86m): 7 (8, 9) balls of Rhubarb #107 (A)
- Louet Sales Kidlin Mohair (1/lace weight; 49% linen, 35% kid mohair, 16% nylon; 1¾ oz/50g, 250 yds/228m): 2 (3, 3) skeins of Regimental Red #59 (B)
- Size 8 (5mm) 24" long circular needles (for the Lower Body)
- Size 9 (5.5mm) 24" long circular needles (for the Upper Body and Sleeves)
- Size 9 (5.5mm) knitting needles (for the Front and Neck Trim)
  Adjust needle size if necessary to obtain gauge.
- Stitch markers (m)
- Tapestry needle

GAUGE

16 sts and 20 rows = 4" using Yarn A and smaller needles in St st for lower body

26 sts and 16 rows = 4" using Yarn A and larger needles in Rib Stitch Patt for front trim

18 sts and 18 rows = 4" using Yarn B and larger needles in St st for sleeves and upper body

To save time, take time to check gauge.

STITCH PATTERNS

Stockinette Stitch (St st)

Row 1 (RS): Knit across.

Row 2 (WS): Purl across.

Repeat Rows 1 and 2.

1 x 1 Rib Stitch

Row 1: *K1, p1; repeat from * to end of row.

Repeat Row 1.

SPECIAL NOTE

This garment can be worn in the traditional kimono fashion (opposite) or it can be turned upside down and worn as a bolero-style sweater (page 34). Worn as a sweater, the lower body section becomes a shawl collar and the front trim becomes a tie around the waist.

SKILL LEVEL

Easy

SIZES

Small (Medium, Large).
Instructions are for smallest size, with changes for other sizes noted in parentheses as necessary.

FINISHED MEASUREMENTS

Bust: 34 (38, 42)"
Total length: 18 (19, 20)"

PATTERN NOTES

The Lower Body is made with Yarn A in one rectangular
piece. The Sleeves and Upper Body are worked in one
piece from side to side using Yarn B. The ribbed trim
on the Front and Neck is made with Yarn A.

LOWER BODY (Right and Left Front, and Back)

With smaller needles and Yarn A, CO 130 (136, 150) sts.
Knit in St st for 11 (12, 13)". Bind off.

UPPER BODY (Back, Right and Left Front, and Sleeves)

With larger needles and Yarn B, CO 110 (120, 128) sts
and work in St st until piece measures 12 (12½, 13)"
from CO edge.

Place markers at each edge, and continue in St st until
piece measures 18 (19, 20)" from CO edge, ending with
a WS row.

Next Row (RS): BO 55 (60, 64) sts and continue working on
next 55 (60, 64) sts until piece measures 4 (4¼, 4½)".

Place marker at the right-hand edge to indicate neck center. Work in St st until neck measures 8 (8½, 9)", ending
with a RS row.

Next Row (WS): Purl 55 (60, 64) sts, then CO 55 (60, 64) sts,
for a total of 110 (120, 128) sts.

Continue in St st for 6 (6½, 7)". Place markers at each
edge. Continue in St st for 12 (12½, 13)" from the new
CO. BO loosely.

FRONT AND NECK TRIM

With larger needles and Yarn A, CO 26 sts. Work in Rib
Stitch Patt until piece measures 56 (58, 60)" from CO
edge. BO in Rib Stitch Patt.

FINISHING

Fold the Upper Body in half and sew right sleeve together
from CO edge to the first markers at point A. Sew the
left sleeve together from BO edge to the last markers at
point B.

Beginning at the right front edge, evenly space, then
join, the BO edge of the Lower Body to the Right Front,
Back, and Left Front of the Upper Body, matching point
A to point A, and point B to point B.

Fold the Front and Neck Trim in half and pin to the center back neck at marker. Join the trim to the neck edge
and along each front, leaving approx. 7" open at the
bottom.

Block lightly.

chrysanthemum

kimono-style cardigan

UPPER BODY SECTION

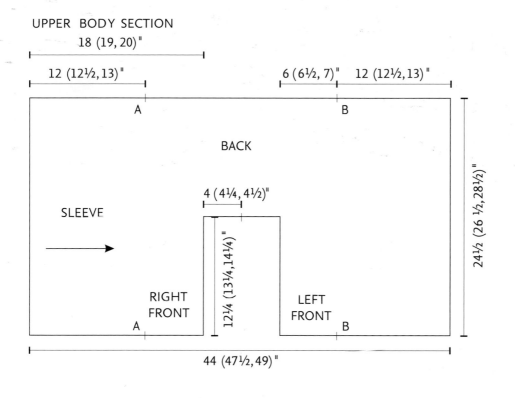

18 (19, 20)"

12 (12½, 13)"

6 (6½, 7)" 12 (12½, 13)"

A B

BACK

4 (4¼, 4½)"

SLEEVE

12¼ (13¼, 14¼)"

RIGHT FRONT

LEFT FRONT

A B

24½ (26 ½, 28½)"

44 (47½, 49)"

LOWER BODY SECTION

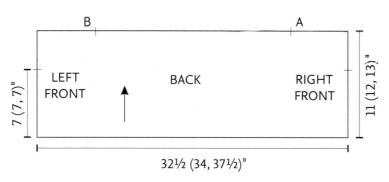

B A

LEFT FRONT

BACK

RIGHT FRONT

7 (7, 7)"

11 (12, 13)"

32½ (34, 37½)"

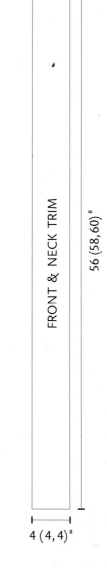

FRONT & NECK TRIM

56 (58, 60)"

4 (4, 4)"

 = Direction of work

clear water *lacy scarf*

I've always enjoyed knitting lace. It feels like playing a game: following special rules, creating an intricate labyrinth, weaving a spider web. My only concern was that I didn't want the scarf to look like my grandmother's doily; I wanted to wear it, not to cover a table with it. My goal was to create a modern, simple, and wearable piece in lace. The result is a light, lacy scarf that reminds me of the clear water of a river, a symbol of rebirth and new life. The modern diagonal eyelet pattern in linen-mohair yarn with crochet trim looks simple and beautiful.

GAUGE

14 sts and 14 rows = 4" in Lace Patt (after blocking)

To save time, take time to check gauge.

STITCH PATTERN

Lace Pattern (multiples of 7 + 2)

Row 1: K2, place marker (pm), *yo, sl 1, k1, psso, k5, repeat from * to last 4 sts, yo, k2tog, pm, k2.

Row 2 (and all even rows): K2, p to last 2 sts, k2.

Row 3: K2, *yo, k1, sl 1, k1, psso, k4, repeat from* to last 4 sts, yo, k2tog, k2.

Row 5: K2, *yo, k2, sl 1, k1, psso, k3, repeat from* to last 4 sts, yo, k2tog, k2.

Row 7: K2, *yo, k3, sl 1, k1, psso, k2, repeat from* to last 4 sts, yo, k2tog, k2.

Row 9: K2, *yo, k4, sl 1, k1, psso, k1, repeat from* to last 4 sts, yo, K2tog, k2.

Row 11: K2, *yo, k5, sl 1, k1, psso, repeat from* to last 4 sts, yo, k2tog, k2.

Row 12: K2, p to last 2 sts, k2.

SCARF

CO 34 sts. Begin Lace Patt.

Repeat Lace Patt until scarf measures 76" long.

BO all sts.

FINISHING

With RS facing, attach yarn and use size G (4mm) crochet hook to single crochet all scarf edges. Block thoroughly.

SKILL LEVEL

Intermediate

FINISHED MEASUREMENTS

9" x 76"

MATERIALS

- Louet Sales KidLin Lace (0/lace weight; 49% linen, 35% kid mohair, 16% nylon; 1¾ oz/50g, 250 yds/228m): 1 skein of Colorado Spruce
- Size 7 (4.5mm) knitting needles
- Size G (4mm) crochet hook
- Stitch markers

morning glory
casual sweater with asymmetric lapel

This sweater is a unique blend of Eastern and Western sensibilities. It has the asymmetry of a single ribbed collar lapel; an ombré effect created by knitting with two yarns held together, a wool yarn and a cotton-linen blend; and decorative seams that emphasize its shape. This standard-fitting pullover is worked continuously from back to front, and the sleeves are constructed by picking up stitches along the armhole edge and working from the top down.

MATERIALS
- Louet Gems (4/medium weight; 100% merino wool; 3½ oz/100g, 175 yds/160m): 5 (6, 6) skeins of Aqua #48 (A)
- Habu Textiles A-144 (1/super-fine weight; 35% cotton, 15% linen, 30% nylon, 20% polyester; 1 oz/28g, 466 yds/426m): 3 cones Lt. Gray #5 (B)
- One each of sizes 6 and 8 (4mm and 5mm) 24" long circular needles. *Adjust needle size if necessary to obtain the correct gauge.*
- Tapestry needle
- Stitch holders

GAUGE
16 sts and 22 rows = 4" in St st using larger needles
To save time, take time to check gauge.

STITCH PATTERNS
Stockinette Stitch (St st)
Row 1 (RS): Knit across.
Row 2 (WS): Purl across.
Repeat Rows 1 and 2.

1 x 1 Rib Stitch
Row 1: *K1, p1. Repeat from * to end of row.
Repeat Row 1.

BACK
With larger needle and two yarns held together, CO 68 (76, 82) sts. Work in St st until piece meas 16 (16½, 17)".

Armhole Shaping
Bind off 3 (4, 4) sts at the beg of next 2 rows. Continue in St st until armhole measures 8½ (9, 9½)" from BO sts.

SKILL LEVEL
Easy

SIZES
Small (Medium, Large).
Instructions are for smallest size, with changes for other sizes noted in parentheses as necessary.

FINISHED MEASUREMENTS
Bust: 34 (38, 40)"
Total length: 24½ (25½, 26½)"

Shoulder and Neck Shaping

Row 1: K 15 (17, 20) sts and place them on a st holder for right front stitches. K to end of row.

Row 2: P 15 (17, 20) sts and place them on a st holder for left front stitches.

Work the center 32 (34, 34) sts in St st for the back neck collar until it meas 3 (3½, 3½)" from the beg ending with WS row. Bind off collar sts keeping the yarn attached.

LEFT FRONT

Using the same strand of yarn pick up 1 st at point B and BO last collar st. Continue to pick up and knit 16 (18, 19) more sts from the side of the back collar (point B to point A). Continue to knit the 15 (17, 20) sts from the left shoulder stitch holder for a total of 32 (36, 40) st. Work in St st for 7" and CO 1 st at the beg of RS row (point C on neck edge). This marks where you will sew the fronts together. Continue working for 1 (1½, 2)". CO 4 (5, 5) sts at the end of the next RS row for underarm shaping. 37 (42, 46) sts.

Continue in St st until it meas 24 (25, 26)" from center shoulder.

RIGHT FRONT

Attach yarn to armhole edge of Right Front next to st holder and knit the 15 right front stitches from the st holder. Continue by picking up 17 (18, 20) sts along side of back collar (point A to point B). Work in St st for 7" and CO 1 st at the end of RS row (point C on neck edge). This marks where you will sew the fronts together. Continue working for 1 (1½, 2)". CO 4 (5, 5) sts at the beg of the next RS row for underarm shaping. 37 (42, 46) sts. Continue as for Left front.

SLEEVES

Pick up and knit 64 (68, 72) sts evenly along armhole edges, not including the BO sts. Work in St st decreasing 1 st each side every 6th row until 13 (14, 15) decreases have been worked. Work even until sleeve measures 16 (16½, 17)". Bind off.

FINISHING

With WS facing, sew Left and Right Fronts together from bottom up (D to C), leaving 7" for neck opening. Using a mattress stitch technique, sew one stitch in from the edge creating a decorative front seam. Sew side seams together using the same decorative seam.

With RS facing sew sleeves from cuff to armhole using the same mattress stitch.

LAPEL

With smaller needles and RS facing pick up and k36 sts starting at the edge of left back collar (point B) continuing 7" down along the left front to point C. Work in 1 x 1 rib slipping 1st st of each row for a smooth edge. Continue rib patt for 5". Bind off.

morning glory

casual sweater with asymmetric lapel

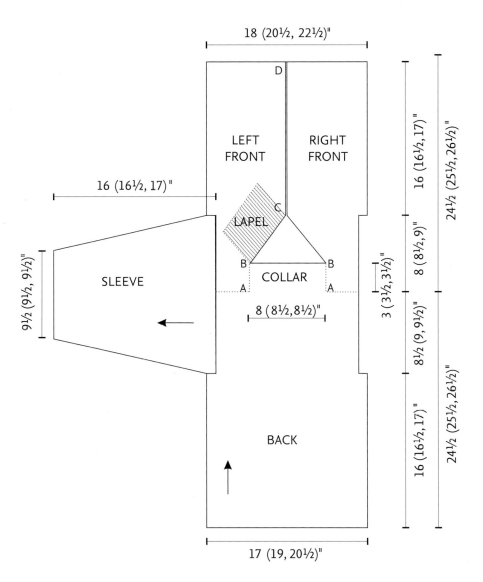

18 (20½, 22½)"

D

LEFT
FRONT

RIGHT
FRONT

16 (16½, 17)"

16 (16½, 17)"

24½ (25½, 26½)"

C

LAPEL

8 (8½, 9)"

9½ (9½, 9½)"

SLEEVE

B

B

3 (3½, 3½)"

COLLAR

A

A

8 (8½, 8½)"

8½ (9, 9½)"

BACK

16 (16½, 17)"

24½ (25½, 26½)"

17 (19, 20½)"

↑ = Direction of work

half-moon rising *two-color vest*

Sometimes yarn speaks to me in its harmony of colors and true artistry in the blending of hues and beautiful fibers. This particular yarn, with its enchanting colors on a background of simple gray, recalls a half-moon rising. It makes this vest look like a work of art. The vest is constructed from only two pieces: The Left Front and Back are knitted as one piece, while the vibrant Right Front is knitted sideways in a rib stitch.

MATERIALS

- Rowan Cocoon (5/bulky weight; 80% merino wool, 20% kid mohair; 3½ oz/100g, 126 yds/115m): 4 (5, 5) balls of Alpine #802 (A)
- Noro Kochoran (5/bulky weight; 50% wool, 30% angora, 20% silk; 3½ oz/100g, 176 yds/161m): 1 skein of #13 (B) as shown here, or #63, #65, or #66
- One each of sizes 9 and 10½ (5.5mm and 6.5mm) 24" long circular needles. *Adjust needle size if necessary to obtain the correct gauge.*
- Stitch holders
- Tapestry needle
- Size F (3.75mm) crochet hook
- One ½" flat button
- One decorative wood button, approx. 2" long

GAUGE

14 sts and 20 rows = 4" in St st using Yarn A on size 10½ (6.5mm) needle
14 sts and 18 rows = 4" in 2 x 3 rib using Yarn B on size 10½ (6.5mm) needle
To save time, take time to check gauge.

STITCH PATTERNS

Garter Stitch
Pattern Row: Knit across.
Repeat Patt Row.

Stockinette Stitch (St st)
Row 1 (RS): Knit across.
Row 2 (WS): Purl across.
Repeat Rows 1 and 2.

2 x 3 Rib Stitch
Row 1 (RS): K2, p3.
Row 2 (WS): K3, p2.
Repeat Rows 1 and 2.

SKILL LEVEL

Easy

SIZES

Small (Medium, Large).
Instructions are for smallest size, with changes for other sizes noted in parentheses as necessary.

FINISHED MEASUREMENTS

Bust: 34 (36, 38)"
Total length: 23 (24½, 25½)"

riverbed

long-sleeve pullover with shawl collar

Regally elegant, a timeless classic, *and a great addition to any wardrobe, this pullover is knit in a deep blue, with the large shawl collar, slightly flared ribbed bottom edge, and sleeve cuffs in a steel gray. The subtle changes in color add to its feminine appeal, and remind me of the water and rocks in a riverbed. The sweater is standard fitting and uses traditional construction and only two basic stitch patterns.*

MATERIALS

- Rowan Kidsilk Haze (3/lightweight; 70% Super Kid Mohair, 30% Silk, 0.88 oz/25g; 229 yds/209m): 4 (4, 5) balls of Hurricane #632 — Yarn A (MC) and 2 (2, 3) balls of Anthracite #639 — Yarn B (CC)
- Habu Textiles A-111 Tsumugi Silk (2/fine weight; 100% silk; 1 oz/28g, 78 yds/71m): 1 ball of Gray #2 — Yarn C (edge trim)
- One each of sizes 6 and 9 (4mm and 5.5mm) 24" long circular needles. *Adjust needle size if necessary to obtain the correct gauge.*
- Stitch holders
- Tapestry needle
- One ⅝" decorative button
- Size F (3.75 mm) crochet hook

GAUGE

16 sts and 22 rows = 4" in St st on larger needles

26 sts and 36 rows = 4" in 2 x 2 Rib on smaller needles

To save time, take time to check gauge.

STITCH PATTERNS

Stockinette Stitch (St st)

Row 1 (RS): Knit across.

Row 2 (WS): Purl across.

Repeat Rows 1 and 2.

2 x 2 Rib Stitch (multiple of 4)

Row 1: *K2, p2. Rep from *.

Repeat this row.

BACK

With CC and smaller needles, CO 132 (148, 164) sts. Work Rib Stitch Patt for 19 rows.

Row 20: *K2tog, p2tog. * Repeat to end for a total of 66 (74, 82) sts.

With MC and larger needles, work in St st until piece measures 14 (15, 16)".

SKILL LEVEL

Easy

SIZES

Small (Medium, Large).

Instructions are for smallest size, with changes for other sizes noted in parentheses as necessary.

FINISHED MEASUREMENTS

Bust: 34 (38, 42)"

Total length: 24½ (26, 27½)"

Armbole Shaping

BO 5 (6, 7) sts at beg of next 2 rows. Dec 1 st each side, every other row, 3x (5x, 6x). Continue in St st until piece measures 22 (23½, 25)" from CO edge.

Back Neck and Shoulder Shaping

Bind off 4 sts at the beg of next 2 rows.

Work 9 sts, attach a second ball of yarn and bind off 24 (26, 30) center back neck sts. Complete row. Working both sides at the same time, BO 4 sts at the shoulder edge once more, then BO remaining 5 sts.

FRONT

Work as for back, including all shaping, and at the same time, when piece measures 16½ (17, 17½)", begin neck shaping.

Front Neck and Shoulder Shaping

Work 13 st, then BO center 24 (26, 30) sts, complete the row. WS Purl to neck edge. Attach a new ball of yarn at neck edge (Point A) and purl left front. Work both sides at once in St st until front meas same as back.

At shoulder edge work shaping same as for back. Bind off 4 sts at the beg of next 4 rows. Bind off rem 5 sts at the beg of next 2 rows.

SLEEVES

With CC and smaller needles CO 68 (72, 76) sts. Work in

2 x 2 rib for 9 rows. Row 10 *k2tog, p2tog* repeat to end. Change to MC and larger needles and begin St st.

Sleeve Shaping

Inc 1 st on each side every 6th (4th, 4th) row 9x (5x, 8x), then every 8th (6th, 6th) row 4x (11x, 8x).
Cont in St st until piece meas 17 (17¼, 17½)".

Cap Shaping

Bind off 4 (6, 6) sts each side.
Dec 1 st each side, every row, 3x (5x, 5x)
Dec 1 st each side every other row 10x (13x, 10x).
Bind off 4 (2, 4) sts at the beg of next 4 rows. Bind off rem 10 (12, 14) sts.
Join Front and Back at shoulder using mattress st. Sew sleeve caps into armholes, then sew sleeve and side seams using mattress st. Weave in all ends.

COLLAR

Use CC yarn and smaller needles. With RS facing begin at point A, and going to point B pick up and knit 40 (42, 44) sts along right front side; from point B to point C, pick up and knit 26 (28, 28) sts from the back neck; and from point C to point D, pick up and knit 40 (42, 44) sts along the left front side, then cast on additional 24 (26, 26) sts onto your needle. 130 (138, 142) sts.

Next Row: K2, p2, rib to end, casting on another 24 (26,

26) sts onto your needle at the end of the row. 154 (164, 168) sts. Work in 2 x 2 rib over all sts for 8". BO loosely.

riverbed

long-sleeve pullover with shawl collar

FINISHING

Sew the two cast-on edges of the front collar extensions
in place point D to point A. They overlap each other
with the right collar over the left. Beginning at point D
with MC yarn and size F (3.75mm) crochet hook, work
one row of single crochet along the collar edge for 3".
Chain 6 sts for a button loop and rejoin collar edge,
continuing the row of single crochet and finishing at
point C. With the wrong side of the collar facing you
attach Yarn C to point A of the left collar edge and Sl st
around the entire collar edge ending at point D.

Attach the button approximately 3¼" up and 3¼" in from
point A where button loop is located.

With Yarn C and size F crochet hook Sl st around the bottom edge and both sleeves.

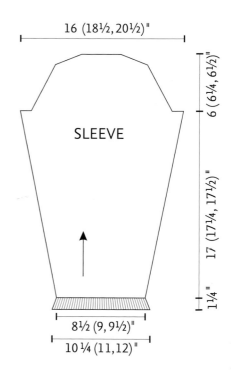

16 (18½, 20½)"

6 (6¼, 6½)"

SLEEVE

17 (17¼, 17½)"

1¼"

8½ (9, 9½)"

10 ¼ (11, 12)"

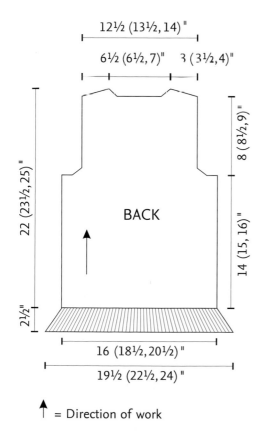

12½ (13½, 14)"

6½ (6½, 7)" 3 (3½, 4)"

8 (8½, 9)"

22 (23½, 25)"

14 (15, 16)"

BACK

2½"

16 (18½, 20½)"

19½ (22½, 24)"

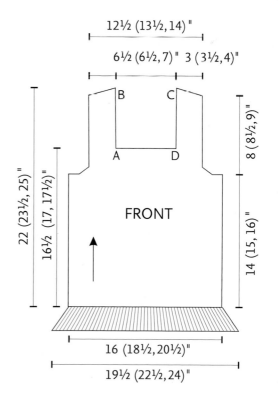

12½ (13½, 14)"

6½ (6½, 7)" 3 (3½, 4)"

B   C

A   D

8 (8½, 9)"

22 (23½, 25)"

16½ (17, 17½)"

14 (15, 16)"

FRONT

16 (18½, 20½)"

19½ (22½, 24)"

↑ = Direction of work

ocean breeze

Summer wind weaving

Sand, sea foam, whitecaps, sea glass

Join swirling wave dance

seaweed   *asymmetric tunic and tie*

Asymmetry, *one of the major components of Japanese aesthetics, lends a fluid dynamic to this tunic. The unusual crimped Japanese cotton yarn, along with the combination of knitted textures, make the piece seem like it's one with nature, or part of the sea. And the seaweedlike tie is just plain fun. Made with only two crochet stitches—a chain stitch and a slipstitch—it is the perfect project for a beginner. It can be worn as a scarf, hair tie, belt, or lariat.*

MATERIALS

- Habu Textiles A-26 Cotton Curl (novelty weight; 100% cotton; 1 oz/28g; 74 yds/68m): 5 (6, 6) balls of Wasabi #2 (A) for the tunic; 1 ball for the tie
- Debbie Bliss Cotton DK (3/lightweight; 100% cotton; 1 3/4 oz/50g; 95 yds/87m, or any other DK 100% cotton in matching color): 1 ball #43 green (B) for the tunic; 1 ball for the tie
- Size 9 (5.5mm) 24" circular needle and size 6 (4mm) straight needles. *Adjust needle size if necessary to obtain the correct gauge.*
- Tapestry needle
- Size H (5mm) crochet hook

GAUGE

For the tunic:

12 sts and 20 rows = 4" in Garter st with Yarn A on larger needle

20 sts and 24 rows = 4" in St st with Yarn B on smaller needle

For the tie:

12 ch = 4" with Yarn A

6 ch = 4" with Yarn B

To save time, take time to check gauge.

STITCH PATTERNS

Garter Stitch

Pattern Row: Knit across.

Repeat Patt Row.

Stockinette Stitch (St st)

Row 1 (RS): Knit across.

Row 2 (WS): Purl across.

Repeat Rows 1 and 2.

SKILL LEVEL

Intermediate

SIZES

Small (Medium, Large).

Instructions are for smallest size, with changes for other sizes noted in parentheses as necessary.

FINISHED MEASUREMENTS

Bust: 36 (38, 40)"

Length of Back: 22½ (24, 25½)"

Tie length: 62"

BACK

With larger needles and Yarn A, CO 54 (58, 60) sts. Work
  in Garter st until piece measures 12 (13, 14)" from CO
  edge, ending with WS row.

Shape Armholes

BO 3 sts at beg of next 2 rows. 48 (52, 54) sts.
Dec 1 st at each end of next 2 rows, then on every other
  row 3x, then on foll 6th row 1x. 36 (40, 42) sts remain.
Work even until armhole measures 6 (6½, 7)".

Shape Back Neck

K 12 sts and place rem sts on st holder.
**Work these 12 sts for right side of back. Dec 1 st at
  neck edge every row 4 times, then every other row 2
  times. 6 sts. Work 1 row. BO rem 6 sts.
With RS facing rejoin yarn to sts on st holder, BO center
  12 (16, 18) sts, k to end. 12 sts. Complete to match first
  side from **.

FRONT

With Yarn A and larger needles CO 54 (56, 58) sts. Work
  in Garter st as follows:
Row 1 (RS): K 4, turn.
Row 2 (WS) and Every Even Row: Sl 1, K to end.
Row 3: K1, M1, k6, turn.
Row 5: K11, turn.
Row 7: K1, M1, k13, turn.
Row 9: K18, turn.
Row 11: K1, M1, k20, turn.
Row 13: K25, turn.
Row 15: K1, M1, k27, turn.
Row 17: K32, turn.
Row 19: K1, M1, k34, turn.
Row 21: K39, turn.
Row 23: K1, M1, k41, turn.
Row 25: K46, turn.
Row 27: K1, M1, k48, turn.
Row 29: K53, turn.
Row 31: K1, M1, k55, turn.
Row 33: K1, k59, turn.
Row 35: K62.

Dec 1 st at the beg of every row until 56 (60, 64) sts rem.
Work even until piece measures 11 (12, 13)" from the
  right bottom edge.

Begin Front Slope Shaping

Next Row (WS): K1, k2tog, knit to end. Continue dec 1 st at
  the same edge on every row, and at the same time after
  5 dec begin armhole shaping for the Left side.

Shape Left Armhole

Next Row (RS): BO 3, k to the last 3 sts, k2tog, k1. Dec 1
  st at armhole edge of next 4 rows, then foll 6th row 1x,
  then on 4th row 1x. K 1 row even while continuing to
  dec 1st on every row at the right front slope.
Work front slope decs until 10 sts remain, then dec 1 st
  on the 4th, 6th, and 8th rows. BO rem 7 sts.

UPPER RIGHT FRONT

With smaller needles and Yarn B CO 2 sts Work in St st
  throughout as follows;
Row 1: Knit 2 sts.
Row 2: P1, M1, p1.
Row 3: K3.
Row 4: P1, M1, p to end.
Continue to inc 1 st as established, until a total of 16 (18,
  20) sts are worked on the Knit row.

Shape Armhole and Neck Edge

Next Row (WS): Continue in St st and BO 4 sts at beg of
  the row (armhole edge) and inc 1 st at end of this row
  (neck edge), 13 (15, 17) sts.
Inc 1 st at beg of next row (neck edge), 14 (16, 18) sts.
Dec 1 st at armhole edge on the next 5 rows, then on 7th
  row 1x, then on foll 4th row 1x.
At same time continue to inc 1 st at the end of the row
  (neck edge). Ending after a right side row. 26 (28, 30)
  sts.
Working armhole straight, dec 1 st at beg of every Knit
  row until 9 sts rem. Work even 3 rows, ending after a
  WS row. BO rem 9 sts.

ASYMMETRIC POCKET

With smaller needles and Yarn B, CO 8 sts. Work in St
   st, increasing 1 st at the beg of every RS row and at the
   end of every other RS row, up to 30 sts. BO.

FINISHING

Assemble all pieces using the mattress stitch.
Attach pocket to left side of front.

TIE

With Yarn A and size H (5mm) crochet hook, chain 93.
   This is your base chain.
Fasten off.
Attach Yarn B and * Sl st into 3 base ch sts; ch 3 into 4th
   st of the base chain; Sl st down the 3 ch sts just made;
   Sl st into next 3 base ch sts, ch 5 into 4th st of the base
   chain; Sl st down the 5 ch sts just made; Sl st into next
   3 base ch sts; ch 7 into 4th st of the base chain; Sl st
   down the 7 ch sts just made.
Repeat from * to the last 3 base ch sts, Sl st into the last 3
   base ch sts. Fasten off.

seaweed

asymmetric tunic and tie

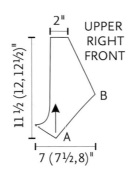

2"

UPPER
RIGHT
FRONT

11½ (12, 12½)"

B

A

7 (7½, 8)"

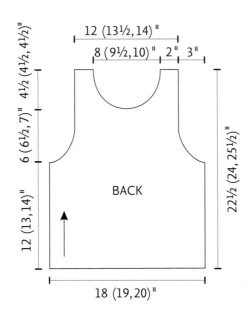

12 (13½, 14)"

8 (9½, 10)" 2" 3"

4½ (4½, 4½)"

6 (6½, 7)"

BACK

12 (13, 14)"

22½ (24, 25½)"

18 (19, 20)"

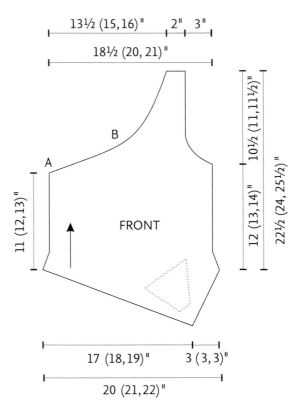

13½ (15, 16)" 2" 3"

18½ (20, 21)"

B

A

11 (12, 13)"

FRONT

10½ (11, 11½)"

12 (13, 14)"

22½ (24, 25½)"

17 (18, 19)" 3 (3, 3)"

20 (21, 22)"

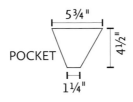

5¾"

POCKET

4½"

1¼"

↑ = Direction of work

coral reef *floaty cap-sleeve pullover*

The loose and airy mesh top, *a quick summer project, is worked from side to side in a simple Garter stitch with a slit in the knitting for the neck opening. The nubby texture of the cotton-silk yarn resembles a coral reef, and the open knit makes the top appropriate for beach weather.*

MATERIALS

- Habu Textiles A-23 (3/lightweight; 45% cotton, 38% silk, 13% twill woven; ½ oz/14g; 46 yds/42m): 5 (6, 6) balls of Orange Red #6
- Size 17 (12.75mm) straight or circular needles. *Adjust needle size if necessary to obtain the correct gauge.*
- Stitch markers
- One tapestry needle
- Size H (5mm) crochet hook

GAUGE

8 sts and 12 rows = 4" in Garter st

To save time, take time to check gauge.

STITCH PATTERNS

Garter Stitch

Pattern Row: Knit across.

Repeat Patt Row.

PULLOVER

CO loosely 33 (34, 36) sts, place marker (pm), CO another 33 (34, 34) sts, for a total of 66 (68, 70) sts.

Work even for 6 (6½, 7)", approx 18 (19, 21) rows.

Neck Opening

Note: Work back and front sections at the same time using 2 balls of yarn.

Next Row (RS): Work to m, attach second ball of yarn, BO 1 st, complete row.

Next Row (WS): Work to 2 sts before neck opening, k2tog.

Work 16 (18, 19) rows of back and front, ending on a WS row.

SKILL LEVEL

Easy

SIZES

Small (Medium, Large).

Instructions are for smallest size, with changes for other sizes noted in parentheses as necessary.

FINISHED MEASUREMENTS

Bust: 34 (36, 40)"

Total length: 16½ (17, 18)"

Neck Closing

Work to 1 st before m, inc 1 st in the last st. With the
same yarn inc 1 in the next st. Work to end 66 (68, 72)
sts. Cut second ball of yarn and work even for 6 (6½,
7)" [18, 19, 21 rows]
BO all sts loosely.

FINISHING

Fold the piece in half widthwise; match points A with A
and B with B. Join sides together from bottom up to
each point using Sl st crochet with a size H (5mm) crochet hook. Leave approx 9 (10, 11)" for armhole openings. Weave in ends.

coral reef

floaty cap-sleeve pullover

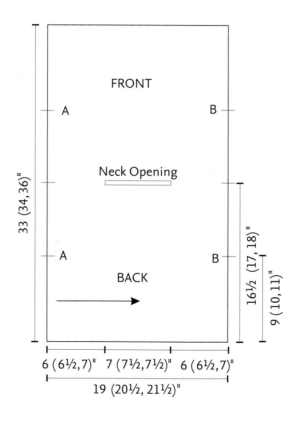

= Direction of work

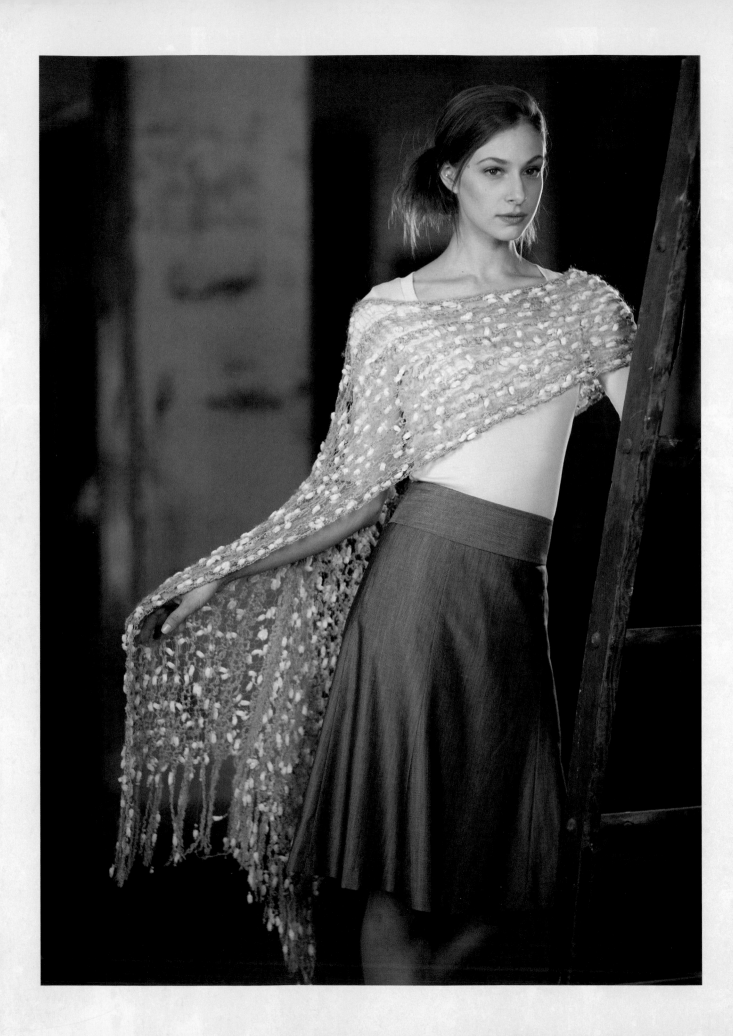

fisherman's net *fringed wrap*

This gossamer wrap gives the impression of lace without the work of making increases, decreases, and yarn overs. You can achieve this effect by using a simple garter stitch and alternating three yarns, each with a beautiful and unique texture. The self fringe is created by leaving a tail of yarn as you change yarns every other row.

MATERIALS

- Habu Textiles A-137 (3/lightweight; 70% silk, 30% cotton; 1 oz/28g; 64 yds/58m): 5 balls of Blue #44 (A)
- Habu Textiles A-29 Tobi Moire (5/bulky weight; 100% polyester; ½ oz/14g; 68 yds/61m): 4 balls of White #1 (B)
- Habu Textiles A-123 Mohair Loop (3/lightweight; 81% mohair, 9% wool, 10% nylon; ½ oz/14 g; 124 yds/113m): 4 balls of Beige #43 (C)
- Size 15 (10mm) 32" or 40" long circular needles.
  Adjust needle size if necessary to obtain the correct gauge.
- Tapestry needle

GAUGE

7 sts and 12 rows = 4" in Garter st
To save time, take time to check gauge.

STITCH PATTERNS

Garter Stitch
Pattern Row: Knit across.
Repeat Patt Row.

WRAP

With Yarn A CO 86 sts leaving a 6" tail.
Note: Leave a 6" tail as you change yarns every 2 rows, on the same side.
This will create a fringe on one side of the shawl.
Work yarns every 2 rows in following order:
Rows 1–2: Knit with A.
Rows 3–4: Knit with B.
Rows 5–6: Knit with A.
Rows 7–8: Knit with C.
Rows 9–10: Knit with B.
Rows 11–12: Knit with A.

SKILL LEVEL

Easy

SIZES

One size fits all

FINISHED MEASUREMENTS

13" x 76" (before seaming)

fisherman's net
fringed wrap

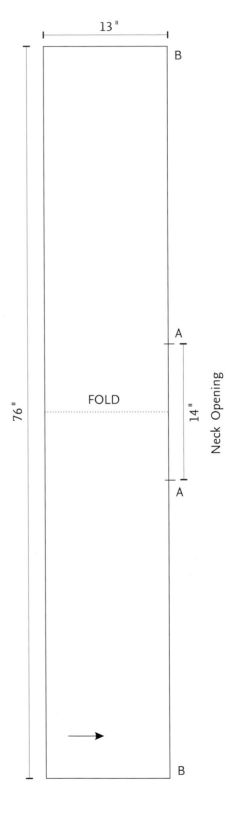

13"

B

A

76"

FOLD

14"

Neck Opening

A

B

↑ = Direction of work

Rows 13–14: Knit with B.

Rows 15–16: Knit with C.

Rows 17–18: Knit with B.

Repeat rows 5–18 one more time.

Next row: Attach Yarn A, leaving a 6" tail. Knit 2 rows.

FINISHING

Attach Yarn C leaving 6" tail, BO all sts except for last 6.
    Pull the yarn through the stitch on the right needle and
    make a knot, and leaving your last 6 sts unknit. Pull the
    needle out and unravel last 6 sts. You will have 6" loops.
    Cut them in half to make the fringe for the second side
    of your shawl.

Fold shawl in half and seam with a mattress stitch along
    the BO edge, matching points A and B and leaving 14"
    for neck opening.

Block lightly to straighten the unraveled fringe.

sand dollar *simple summer tank*

White linen yarn reminds me of childhood summers with my parents in Crimea, on the beautiful white sand beaches of the Black Sea. I felt that white linen was not enough by itself, though; it needed a touch of something else. I added a thin cotton-linen yarn for more depth and life. As I created this summer tank, my memories were vivid: memories of sand slipping through my fingers, of shells and small rocks and blue water, of feeling peaceful and carefree. The tank is close-fitting and knit in one piece. Although construction is simple, it has an off-center slit and a decorative back seam. Worked in Stockinette stitch, this piece is fun to knit.

MATERIALS

- Louet Euroflax Originals (2/fine; 100% linen; 3½ oz/100g, 270 yds/247m): 2 (2, 3) skeins of White #70 (A)
- Habu Textiles A-144 (1/super-fine weight; 35% cotton, 15% linen, 30% nylon, 20% polyester; 1 oz/28g, 466 yds/426m): 2 (2,3) cones of Lt. Grey #5 (B)
- One each of sizes 6 and 7 (4mm and 4.5mm) 24" long circular needles. *Adjust needle size if necessary to obtain the correct gauge.*
- Tapestry needle
- Two stitch holders
- Three ⅞" decorative buttons

GAUGE

20 sts and 22 rows = 4" in St st on larger needles with both strands of yarn
To save time, take time to check gauge.

STITCH PATTERNS

Stockinette Stitch (St st)
Row 1 (RS): Knit across.
Row 2 (WS): Purl across.
Repeat Rows 1 and 2.

2 x 2 Rib Stitch (even number of sts)
Row 1 (RS): K2, p2, repeat across.
Row 2 (WS): Knit the knit sts, purl the purl sts.
Repeat Rows 1 and 2.

PATTERN NOTE

For a beautiful added detail, you can drop Yarn B over the 4 armhole edge and neck stitches as well as on the front straps.

SKILL LEVEL

Easy

SIZES

Small (Medium, Large).
Instructions are for smallest size, with changes for other sizes noted in parentheses as necessary.

FINISHED MEASUREMENTS

Bust: 34 (38, 40)"
Total length: 21½ (22½, 24½)"

RIGHT BACK

With smaller needles and 1 strand of Yarn A and 1 strand of B held together CO 66 (72, 76) sts. Work in 2 x 2 rib for 1", ending with a WS row. Change to larger needles and work in St st for 5½", ending with a WS row.

FRONT AND LEFT BACK

With smaller needles and 1 strand of Yarn A and 1 strand of B held together CO 110 (120, 130) sts. Work in 2 x 2 rib for 1" ending with the WS row. Change to larger needles work in St st for 5½" to match the Right Back ending with a WS row.

Knit stitches of Left Back and Front and using the same strand of yarn continue to knit the Right Back stitches from the stitch holder joining both sections.

Work even 176 (192, 206) sts in St st until piece meas 14½ (15, 15½)" from CO edge. End with a WS row.

Divide Left Back

Knit 44 (50, 53) sts. Place foll 88 (92, 100) sts for the Front on a stitch holder. Place rem 44 (50, 53) sts for the Right Back on a second stitch holder.

Work 44 (50, 53) Left Back sts in St st for 3 rows.

Underarm Shaping

Row 1 (Decrease Row) (RS): Knit to the last 8 sts, k2tog, k2tog, k4.

Row 2 (and all even rows): Purl.

Repeat these 2 rows 3 times.

Repeat Row 1 every 4th row 7 more times. Work even until work meas 8 (8½, 9)" from the armhole. BO all sts.

Upper Right Back

Attach yarn at center back edge (point A) and p44 (50, 53) Right Back sts from the st holder. Work 2 more rows of St st.

Row 1 (Decrease Row) (RS): K4, ssk, ssk, k to end.

Row 2 (and all even rows): Purl.

Repeat these 2 rows 3 times. Repeat Row 1 every 4th row 7 more times. Work even until work meas 8 (8½, 9)" from the armhole. BO all sts.

Upper Right Front

Transfer Front sts from st holder to needle.

With RS facing attach yarn (point B) and k35 (37, 40) Left Front sts. Bind off 18 (20, 22) center front sts and knit last 35 (37, 40) Right Front sts. Return Left Front 35 (37, 40) sts to st holder. Working the Right Front sts, purl 1 row.

Right Front Neck and Armhole Shaping

Row 1 (Decrease Row) (RS): K4, ssk, knit to the last 8 sts, k2tog, k2tog, k4.

Row 2 (WS): Purl.

Repeat Rows 1 and 2 twice more. Continue decreases as follows:

Neck Shaping: At neck edge: K4, ssk on every RS row 5x (6x, 7x), then every other RS row 3x (4x, 4x). At the same time continue at Armhole edge: K2tog, k2tog, k4 on every other RS row 4x (4x, 5x).

When final neck edge decreases have been worked: K4, k2tog, k4. 9 sts

Work even on 9 sts in St st for 7½ (8, 8¼)". BO.

Upper Left Front

Attach yarn at point B and work Left front as Right Front beginning with Row 1, reversing all shaping. (Work k4, k2tog at neck edge instead of ssk; and ssk, ssk, k4 instead of k2tog, k2tog, k4 at the armhole edge.)

FINISHING

Block lightly.

Holding the wrong side of the back sections together, sew the center seam 1 stitch back from the edge creating a decorative seam on the outside of the garment. Sew neck strap ends together. Match the strap seam to the center back seam and using the same decorative seam technique sew the left and right strap along the back of the garment. Weave in all ends.

Beginning at the top of the front slit, attach each of the decorative buttons 1½" apart.

sand dollar

simple summer tank

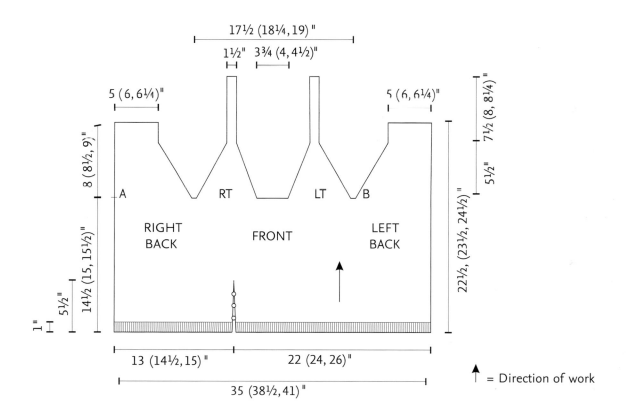

17½ (18¼, 19)"

1½"   3¾ (4, 4½)"

5 (6, 6¼)"   5 (6, 6¼)"

7½ (8, 8¼)"

8 (8½, 9)"

5½"

A   RT   LT   B

RIGHT BACK   FRONT   LEFT BACK

22½, (23½, 24½)"

14½ (15, 15½)"

5½"

1"

13 (14½, 15)"   22 (24, 26)"

35 (38½, 41)"

↑ = Direction of work

fading light

City never sleeps

Sundown, dusk, alluring lights

Excitement beckons

hazy moon *ethereal scarf*

Since cherry blossoms and a hazy moon sometimes coincide, some believe that the beauty of these blossoms causes the moon to become hazy or to blush. But actually the haze around the moon is associated with warmth. This made me think of designing a scarf, made with fragile flowerlike yarn, to look like a weightless veil of haze surrounding the neck. A beautiful combination of yarns made it possible to achieve a truly gossamer effect.

MATERIALS

- Habu Textiles A-62 paper moiré (3/lightweight; 50% linen, 50% nylon; 1oz/28g; 311 yds/284m): 1 ball of Mocha #5 (A)
- Habu Textiles A-67 fringe tape ribbon (novelty yarn; 100% acetate; ½ oz/14g; approx. 7 yds/6.4m): 1 ball of Gray #3 (B)
- One pair size 13 (9mm) knitting needles.
  Adjust needle size if necessary to obtain the correct gauge.

GAUGE

11 sts and 18 rows = 4" in Garter st in Yarn A
To save time, take time to check gauge.

STITCH PATTERN

Garter Stitch
Pattern Row: Knit across.
Repeat Patt Row.

PATTERN NOTE

Leave 3" tails every time you begin and end Yarn A and Yarn B. Use any adhesive bond or fabric glue to prevent the edges from fraying.

SCARF

With B, CO 14 sts. Cut ribbon, leaving a 3" tail.
Using A, k 24 rows. Cut yarn, leaving a 3" tail.
Using B, k 1 row. Cut yarn, leaving 3" tail.
Using A, knit to 36" from the CO edge. Cut yarn, leaving a 3" tail.
Using B, k 1 row. Cut ribbon, leaving a 3" tail.
Using A, k 24 rows. Cut yarn, leaving a 3" tail.
BO using B. Cut ribbon, leaving a 3" tail. Do not weave in any yarn
  or ribbon ends.

SKILL LEVEL

Easy

FINISHED MEASUREMENTS

5" x 42"

evening mist   *simple cropped shift*

Wool—stainless steel yarn reminds me of sculpting when I was in art school. It's so fine and pliable, you have to have an open mind to work with it. It's a new experience, not like knitting with the usual wool yarn. You are creating art that is light and airy and feels like an evening mist. The loose-fitting top, worked with two strands of yarn, shapes to your body. It has a lace detail in the front, and a stretchy boat neck with unique shoulder seaming: The right side is a traditional horizontal seam, while the left side is a vertical seam worked from the top down.

MATERIALS

- Habu Textiles A-148 Wool Stainless Steel (1/super fine weight; 75% wool, 25% stainless steel; ½ oz/14g; 273 yds/250m): 6 (7, 8) cones of Forest #5997
- One pair each of sizes 6 and 9 (4mm and 5.5mm) knitting needles. *Adjust needle size if necessary to obtain the correct gauge.*
- Tapestry needle

GAUGE

26 sts and 28 rows = 4" in St st with smaller needles and 2 strands of yarn held together. *To save time, take time to check gauge.*

STITCH PATTERNS

Stockinette Stitch (St st)
Row 1 (RS): Knit across.
Row 2 (WS): Purl across.
Repeat Rows 1 and 2.

Lace Stitch (multiple of 2 sts +1)
Row 1: K1, *yo, k2tog; rep from * to end.
Row 2: Purl across.
Repeat Rows 1 and 2.

PATTERN NOTE

This garment is knit with 2 strands of yarn held together throughout.

BACK

With smaller needles and 2 strands of yarn held together CO 110 (120, 136) sts and work in St st for 25 (26, 27)". BO loosely.

RIGHT FRONT

CO 30 (34, 40) sts and work in St st for 24 (25, 26)". BO loosely.

SKILL LEVEL

Easy

SIZES

Small (Medium, Large).
Instructions are for smallest size, with changes for other sizes noted in parentheses as necessary.

FINISHED MEASUREMENTS

Bust: 32–34 (36–38, 40–42)"
Total length: 24 (25, 26)"

LEFT FRONT

CO 84 (88, 92) sts and work in St st for 24 (25, 26)". BO loosely.

FINISHING

Sew two front sections together, from A to B, using a mattress stitch.

Sew the right front to the back, from points F to G for the right shoulder seam.

Sew 1½" from top down at point C. This will become the left shoulder seam.

Sew front to back at points D to E, for side seams, 13½ (14, 15½)" from bottom up, leaving space for armholes.

FRONT LACE TRIM

With RS facing using larger needles and 2 strands of yarn held together pick up and knit 74 (78, 82) sts along front seam from neck down. CO 20 additional sts onto needle. 94 (98, 102) sts.

Work Lace st for 3". BO loosely.

evening mist

simple cropped shift

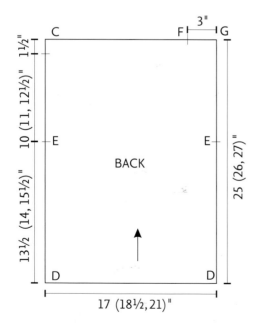
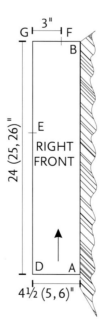
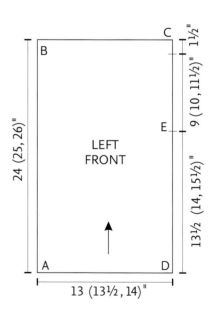

↑ = Direction of work

lantern floating *softly felted top and skirt*

Sometimes beauty shows itself in unexpected ways and is a result of an accidental outcome. For this top and skirt, I used two unusual yarns and then lightly felted the finished garments. The tradition of felting fabrics can be traced back to the early Vikings and Mongols, but the technique is up-to-the-minute and especially interesting with today's yarns. The unique sculptural quality of the silk–stainless steel yarn gives these pieces their incredible ability to shape to your body, while the softness and warmth comes from the wool. From the fusion of unusual yarns and light felting comes two pieces that are romantic, soft, and feminine, with a beautiful wabi-sabi look, the Japanese aesthetic of imperfection.

MATERIALS

For the top:

- Habu Textiles A-21 1/20 Silk Stainless Steel (1/fine weight; 69% silk, 31% stainless steel; ½ oz/14g; 311 yds/284m): 3 (4, 4) cones of Gray #3 (A)
- Habu Textiles Yarn A-177 merino wool (1/fine weight; 100% merino; 1 oz/28g; 747 yds/667m): 2 (2, 2) cones of Brick #45 (B)
- One each sizes 6 and 8 (4mm and 5mm) straight and size 8 (5mm) 24" long circular needles.

For the skirt:

- Habu Textiles A-21 1/20 Silk Stainless Steel (1/fine weight; 69% silk, 31% stainless steel; ½ oz/14g, 311 yds/284m): 4 (5, 5) cones of Gray #3 (A)
- Habu Textiles Yarn A-177 merino wool (1/fine weight; 100% merino; 1 oz/28g, 747 yds/667m): 1 (2, 2) cones of Brick #45 (B)
- One each of sizes 4 and 8 (3.5mm and 5mm) 24" long circular needles. *Adjust needle size if necessary to obtain the correct gauge.*
- Stitch holders
- Tapestry needle
- Size D (3.25mm) crochet hook
- Six ½" flat buttons for the skirt

GAUGE

24 sts and 28 rows = 4" with Yarn A and Yarn B held together in St st on larger needles

24 sts and 30 rows = 4" with 1 strand of Yarn A in St st on size 6 (4mm) needles

26 sts and 32 rows = 4" with 2 strands of Yarn A held together in St st on size 4 (3.5mm) needles

Note that gauge for this pattern is approximate and is not critical.

SKILL LEVEL

Easy

SIZES

Small (Medium, Large).
Instructions are for smallest size, with changes for other sizes noted in parentheses as necessary.

FINISHED MEASUREMENTS

(before felting)

For the top:

Bust: 36 (38, 42)"

Total length: 21 (23½, 25)"

For the skirt:

Waist: 32 (34, 38)"

Total length: 27 (28, 29)"

STITCH PATTERN

Stockinette Stitch (St st)

Row 1 (RS): Knit across.

Row 2 (WS): Purl across.

Repeat Rows 1 and 2.

PATTERN NOTE

It is important to make a swatch before starting your
project. However, keep in mind that these garments
have an approximate gauge due to the nature of these
unusual yarns. As long as the gauge is not too far off,
the elasticity of the yarn should take care of the rest.
Always cast on and bind off loosely.

TOP
BACK

With 1 strand of Yarn A and smaller needles loosely CO
122 (133, 146) sts.

Work in St st. for 2½". Set work aside.

With 1 strand each of Yarn A and Yarn B held together
and larger straight needles, CO 122 (133, 146) sts. Work
in St st for 10 rows.

Next Row: To join pieces, hold larger needle with WS sts
on top of RS sts from smaller needle. Using size 8

(5mm) 24" circular needles, K 1 st from size 8 straight
needles together with 1 st from size 6 straight needle.
122 (133, 146) sts

Work in St st until piece measures 12½ (14, 15½)".

Armhole Shaping

BO 9 (11, 12) sts at beg of next 2 rows.

Dec 1 st each side every other row 8x (10x, 12x).

Cont in St st until piece measures 20½ (23, 24½)" from
CO edge.

Shape Shoulders and Back Neck

BO 7 (7, 8) sts at the beg of next 2 rows. Work 14 (16,
18) sts, attach a second ball of yarn and BO 44 (45, 46)
center back neck sts. Complete row. Working both sides
at the same time, BO 7 (7, 8) shoulder sts and dec 1 st
at each neck edge. BO rem 6 (8, 9) shoulder sts on
each side.

FRONT

Work as for Back, including all shaping, and at the same
time begin neck shaping when piece measures 19
(21½, 23)".

Work 34 (33, 34) sts. Attach another set of yarns and BO
center 20 (25, 30) sts. Complete row. Working both
sides at the same time, BO 2 sts at neck edge 3x.
Dec 1 st at each neck edge every other row 7x (3x, 2x).
While working front neck edge decreases, when piece
meas 20½ (23, 24½)" from CO edge, work shoulder
shaping as for back.

SLEEVES

With 1 strand of Yarn A and smaller needles, loosely CO
72 (78, 78) sts.
Working in St st, dec 1 st each side, every 2nd row 5x (3x,
3x), then every 4th row 2x (0x, 0x). When piece measures
2", set work aside. 58 (72, 72) sts
With 1 strand each of Yarns A and B held together and
larger straight needles, CO 58 (72, 72) sts. Work in St st
for 8 rows.
Next Row: Hold larger needle with WS sts on top of RS sts
from smaller needle. Using circular needles, K 1 st from
size 8 straight needle together with 1 st from size 6
needle. 58 (72, 72) sts.
Next Row (WS): Purl.

Sleeve Shaping

Work 2 more rows ending with WS row.
Inc 1 st on each side every 2nd (4th, 2nd) row 14x (16x,
5x), then every 4th (6th, 4th) row 9x (3x, 18x).
Cont in St st until piece meas 10 (11½, 12)". (104, 110,
118) sts.

Cap Shaping

BO 9 (10, 12) sts at beg of next 2 rows.
Dec 1 st each side every other row, 22x (24x, 26x).
BO 4 sts at the beg of next 4 rows.
BO rem 26 sts.

SCARF–COLLAR

With larger needles and Yarn A, cast on 60 sts. Work in St
st for 30", then change to smaller needles and Yarn B
and continue working in St st for another 16". BO.

FELTING

Felting, agitating knitted pieces in warm to hot water, is a
process that creates a more solid and dense fabric. The
wool yarn will felt because it's an animal fiber, but the
silk-stainless steel yarn will not: The result creates an
interesting texture for the skirt and top.

To felt, gently wash the top-and-scarf and the skirt with its
ties in warm water by hand. Agitate them lightly to create
a felted affect. Be careful not to over felt. The skirt and top
should not shrink more than 5 percent. Let them air dry,
then block them where necessary. You may want to felt a
swatch of the knitting first to see how it reacts.

FINISHING

Join side and shoulder seams. Weave in all ends. Leaving
approximately 4" of the center front open, begin attaching the scarf–collar to the Right Front at point A. Begin
to sew where Yarn A and Yarn B of the scarf meet. The
Yarn B length will be unattached and used as the right
side tie. Continue attaching the Yarn A portion of the
scarf until you have reached point B on the left front,
maintaining the 4" opening. Approximately 7" of the
Yarn A portion of the scarf will remain, to be used as
the left front tie. Felt the top-and-scarf.

lantern floating

softly felted top

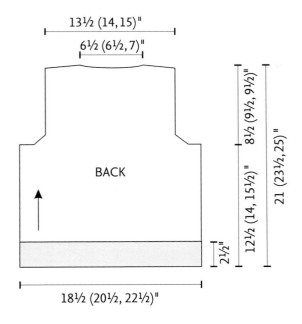

13½ (14, 15)"
6½ (6½, 7)"
BACK
2½"
12½ (14, 15½)"
8½ (9½, 9½)"
21 (23½, 25)"
18½ (20½, 22½)"

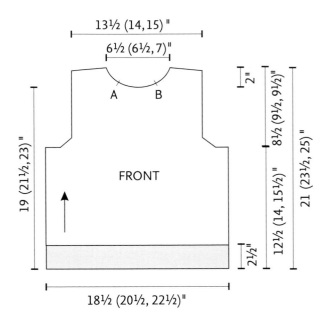

13½ (14, 15)"
6½ (6½, 7)"
2"
A   B
FRONT
19 (21½, 23)"
2½"
12½ (14, 15½)"
8½ (9½, 9½)"
21 (23½, 25)"
18½ (20½, 22½)"

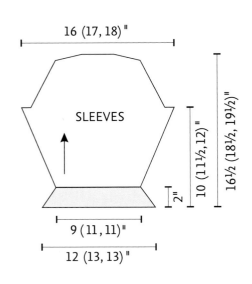

16 (17, 18)"
SLEEVES
2"
10 (11½, 12)"
16½ (18½, 19½)"
9 (11, 11)"
12 (13, 13)"

↑ = Direction of work

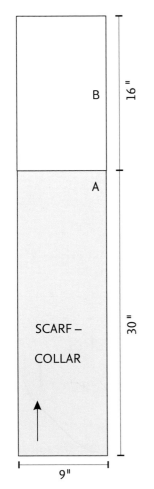

B
16"
A
SCARF –

COLLAR
30"
9"

SKIRT
FRONT AND BACK (same)

With smaller needles and 2 strands of Yarn A, loosely CO 126 (140, 154) sts. Work in Garter st for 4 rows, then change to St st and work for 2½".

Next Row (RS): With 1 strand each of Yarn A and Yarn B held together, change to larger needles and increase (M1) 12 (14, 16) sts evenly spaced across row (every 11 sts). 138 (154, 170) sts. Continue in St st for 10 rows.

Decrease Row (RS): K2, k2tog, knit to the last 4 sts, ssk, k2.

Work this decrease row on every 10th RS row 4x (2x, 0x) – 130 (152, 168) sts; every 8th row 3x (5x, 7x) – 124 (142, 154) sts; every 6th row 2x (3x, 4x) – 120 (136, 146) sts; every 4th row 10x (7x, 6x) – 98 (122, 134) sts. Work even until piece measures 24 (25, 26)" from CO edge.

Change to smaller needles, and with 2 strands of Yarn A held together continue in St st for 2".

Skirt Front Eyelets

Next row (RS): K6 (4, 8) *yo twice, k2tog, k8 (9, 12), repeat from * 3 (4, 3) more times. yo twice, k2tog, k2 (2, 4). *yo twice, k2tog, k8 (9, 12), repeat from * 3 (4, 3) more times, yo twice, k2tog, k4 (2, 8).

Next row (WS): P5 (3, 9), *sl the first loop of the double yo and purl the second loop, p9 (10, 13), repeat from * 3 (4, 3) more times. Sl the first loop of the double yo and purl the second loop, p3 (3, 5). Continue as established, end p6 (4, 8). 96 (122, 134) sts. Continue in St st for 2".

Skirt Back Eyelets

Next row (RS): K8 (5, 4) * yo twice, k2tog, k10 (12, 12), repeat from* 6 (7, 8) more times, yo twice, k2tog, k2 (3, 2).

Next row (WS): P3 (4, 3), * Sl the first loop of the double yarn over and purl the second loop, p11 (13, 13), repeat from * 6 (7, 8) more times. Complete last eyelet as established p8 (5, 4). 96 (122, 134) sts.

Continue in St st for 2".

FINISHING

Use a traditional mattress stitch to sew the sides together. Leave the left side waistband open for buttonhole loops and buttons.

With Yarn A and Yarn B held together and size D (3.25mm) crochet hook, work single crochet st along the open edge of the waistband back. Work from the top down to the skirt as a trim.

Buttonhole Loops

Continue with the same yarns and single crochet up the front waistband edge. Turn and chain 6 sts. Skip 3 edge single crochet stitches and join the loop to the edge working 3 more single crochet. Continue to work in this manner creating 6 buttonhole loops evenly spaced along the front skirt waistband opening.

Attach buttons to correspond with buttonhole loops.

(For an optional simpler finishing, use a traditional mattress stitch to sew the sides together completely. For this finishing, you do not need the buttons.)

WAISTBAND TIES

With size D (3.25mm) crochet hook and 1 strand each of Yarn A and Yarn B held together, crochet three 70" chains. Braid these three ties together making a knot at each end.

Weave braided tie through eyelets and pull both ends of ties through the front center.

FELTING

See the instructions on page 81 to felt the skirt and ties.

lantern floating

softly felted skirt

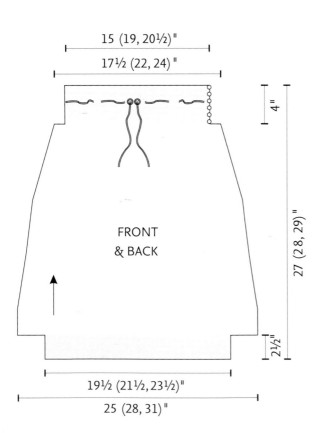

15 (19, 20½)"

17½ (22, 24)"

4"

FRONT
& BACK

27 (28, 29)"

2½"

19½ (21½, 23½)"

25 (28, 31)"

↑ = Direction of work

long night *elegant capelet*

Beautiful as well as unusual, *this elegant capelet is knit with a linen yarn and a metallic rayon held together. The interesting texture comes from a series of stitch patterns that form a kaleidoscope-like image. The unique shape is created by the way the three pieces, two rectangular front-and-sleeve sections and a back insert, are sewn together. Two sizes and an easy fit make this project perfect for everyone. Although the pattern is challenging, when it is worked step by step, this garment is a treat to knit.*

MATERIALS

- Blue Heron Rayon Metallic (3/lightweight; 85% rayon, 15% metallic; 8 oz/226g, 550 yds/503m): 2 skeins of Graphite (A)
- Habu Textiles A-60 Linen Paper (4/medium weight; 100% linen; 2 oz/56g, 560 yds/512m): 2 cones of Charcoal #119 (B)
- Size 8 (5mm) 24" long circular.
  Adjust needle if necessary to obtain the correct gauge.
- Stitch markers
- Tapestry needle
- One 1" flat button
- Size F (3.75mm) crochet hook

GAUGE

16 sts and 24 rows = 4" in St st with yarns A and B held together
To save time, take time to check gauge.

STITCH PATTERNS

Garter Stitch
Pattern Row: Knit across.
Repeat Patt Row.

Stockinette Stitch (St st)
Row 1 (RS): Knit across.
Row 2 (WS): Purl across.
Repeat Rows 1 and 2.

Reverse Stockinette Stitch (rev St st)
Row 1 (RS): Purl across.
Row 2 (WS): Knit across.
Repeat Rows 1 and 2.

SKILL LEVEL

Intermediate to advanced

SIZES

Small/Medium (Medium/Large).
Instructions are for smallest size, with changes for other size noted in parentheses as necessary.

FINISHED MEASUREMENTS

Bust (closed): 32–36 (38–42)"
Total length: 16 (18)"

1 x 1 Rib Stitch Pattern

1 x 1 Rib Stitch Pattern

Row 1: *K1, p1; repeat from * to end of row.

Repeat Row 1.

PATTERN NOTES

This garment is knit in three pieces with 1 strand each of Yarn A and Yarn B held together throughout construction. Two rectangular pieces form the sleeves and upper body and the third piece creates a back insert that is worked in 1 x 1 rib and St st.

It is critical to use stitch markers when making the increases and decreases before or after the specific markers. The number of stitches in the two rectangular pieces remains constant. The charted design (see pages 92–99) is worked from right to left for the odd number right side rows and from left to right for the even number wrong side rows. It's helpful to use a yellow marker to highlight the wrong side rows.

LEFT UPPER BODY AND SLEEVE

First Design Order: Rev St st; St st; Garter; 1 x 1 rib; rev St st.

Stitch Set-Up Row: CO 3 (4) sts, place marker (pm), CO 21 (23) sts, pm, CO 21 (23) sts, pm, CO 4 sts, pm, CO 21 (23) sts, pm, CO 21 (23) sts, pm, CO 3 (4) sts. 96 (104) sts.

Row 1 (RS): P to first m, yo, sl m (slip marker), k to within 2 sts before next m, k2tog, sl m, ssk, k to next m, sl m, yo, k to next m, yo, sl m, 1 x 1 rib to within 2 sts before next m, k2tog, sl m, ssk, 1 x 1 rib to next m, sl m, yo, p to end.

Row 2 (WS): K to first m, sl m, work sts as they face you to next m, sl m, work sts as they face you to next m, sl m, k to the next m, sl m, p to next m, sl m, p to next m, sl m, k to end.

Continue following the charted pattern of the first design order, from Row 3 through Row 38 (42).

Second Design Order: Rev St st; Garter; 1 x 1 rib; St st; rev St st.

Row 1 (RS): P to within 1 st before m, k1, sl m, k to next m, remove m, k to next m, yo, sl m, 1 x 1 rib foll 19 (21) sts, k2tog, pm (place marker), ssk, 1 x 1 rib to next m, sl m, yo, k to next m, remove m, k to next m, sl m, k1, p to end.

Row 2 (WS): K to within 1 st before m, p1, sl m, p to next m, sl m, work sts as they face you to next m, sl m, work sts as they face you to the next m, sl m, k to next marker, sl m, k to end.

Continue following the charted pattern of the second design order, beginning with Row 3 and working through Row 38 (42).

Repeat the first design order one more time beginning with Row 1. Reposition the markers to their original places. Work the charted design through Row 38 (42). BO all sts.

RIGHT UPPER BODY AND SLEEVE

First Design Order: Rev St st; 1 x 1 rib; Garter; St st; rev St st.

CO 3 (4) sts, pm (place marker), CO 21 (23) sts, pm, CO 21 (23) sts, pm CO 4 sts, pm, CO 21 (23) sts, pm, CO 21 (23) sts, pm CO 3 (4) sts. 94 (104) sts

Row 1 (RS): P to first m, yo, sl m (slip marker), 1 x 1 rib to within 2 sts before next m, k2tog, sl m, ssk, 1 x 1 rib to next m, sl m, yo, k to next m, yo, sl m, k within 2 sts before next m, k2tog, sl m, ssk, k to the next m, sl m, yo, p to end.

Row 2 (WS): K to first m, sl m, p to the next m, sl m, p to next m, sl m, k to next m, sl m, work sts as they face you to next m, sl m, work sts as they face you to next m, sl m, k to end.

Continue following the charted pattern beginning with Row 3 through Row 38 (42).

Second Design Order: Rev St st; St st; 1 x 1 rib; Garter; rev St st.

Row 1 (RS): P to within 1 st before m, k1, sl m, k to next m, remove m, k to next m, yo, sl m, 1 x 1 rib foll 19 (21) sts, k2tog, pm (place marker), ssk, 1 x 1 rib to next m, sl m, yo, k to next m, remove marker, k to next m, sl m, k1, p to end.

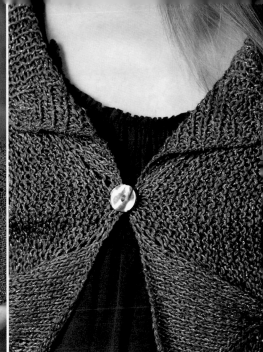

Row 2 (WS): K to m, sl m, k to next m, sl m, work sts as they face you to next m, sl m, work sts as they face you to next m, sl m, p to next m, sl m, p1, k to end.

Continue following the charted pattern of the second design order beginning with Row 3 and work through Row 38 (42).

Repeat the first design order one more time beginning with Row 1. Reposition the markers to their original places. Work the charted design through Row 38 (42). BO all sts.

BACK INSERT

CO 44 sts. Work 1 x 1 rib for 2 rows.

Next row and every 4th row decrease 1 st each side until 34 sts remain.

Change to St st and work 2 rows.

Inc Row (RS): K4, M1, k to last 4 sts, M1, k4.

Continue inc 1 st on each side as established every 4th row until 54 (60) sts.

Work 3 rows even.

Dec Row (RS): K3, ssk, k to last 5 sts, k2tog, k 3 sts.

Dec 1 st on each side every RS row as established until 24 (28) sts.

BO rem sts.

FINISHING

Use a traditional mattress stitch seam to sew the right and left sleeve seams together, beginning at point E and ending at point C. Align back insert points A to B with points A to B of right back section and seam, continuing to point C at the sleeve underarm. Rotating the back insert, seam from the underarm points C to D ending at the back neck edge point D. Repeat the same seaming order for the left back section.

Attach button as shown in the schematic at the lower edge of the Left Front. The first yo on the Right Front is used as the buttonhole.

With a size F (3.75mm) crochet hook and Yarn B, work a row of Reverse Single Crochet around the entire outside edge. (Crochet edge is optional.)

long night

elegant capelet

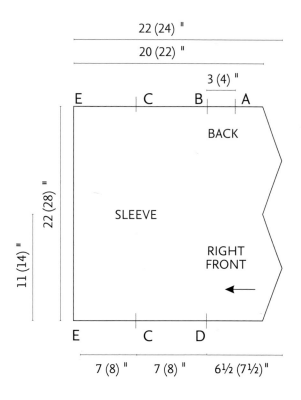

22 (24) "

20 (22) "

3 (4) "

E   C   B   A

BACK

SLEEVE

RIGHT
FRONT

←

22 (28) "

11 (14) "

E   C   D

7 (8) "   7 (8) "   6½ (7½)"

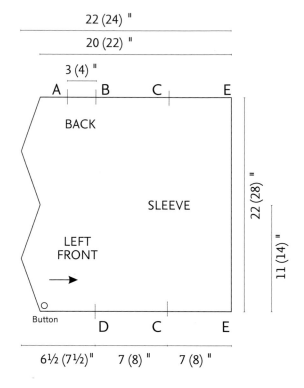

22 (24) "

20 (22) "

3 (4) "

A   B   C   E

BACK

SLEEVE

LEFT
FRONT

→

○ Button

D   C   E

6½ (7½)"   7 (8) "   7 (8) "

22 (28) "

11 (14) "

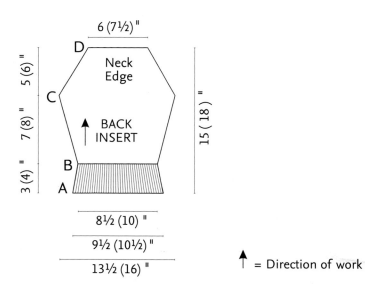

6 (7½) "

D

Neck
Edge

C

↑ BACK
INSERT

B

A

5 (6) "

7 (8) "

3 (4) "

15 (18) "

8½ (10) "

9½ (10½) "

13½ (16) "

↑ = Direction of work

long night

S/M — right upper body & sleeve

Second Design Order

First Design Order

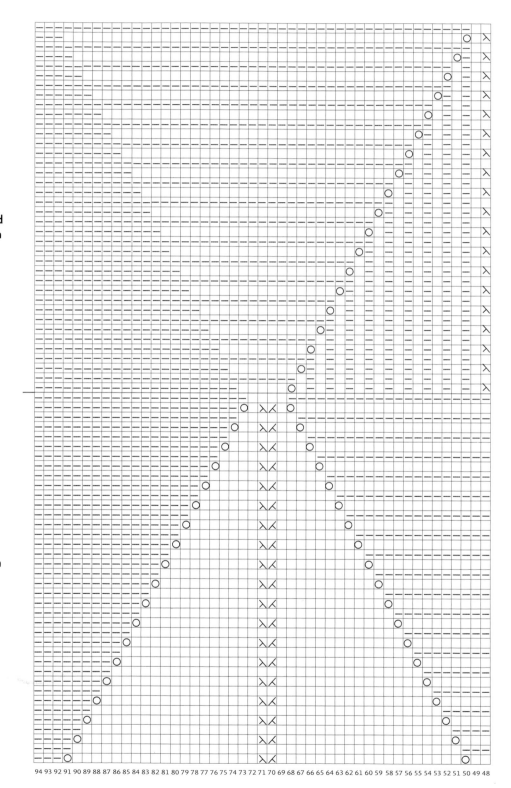

94 93 92 91 90 89 88 87 86 85 84 83 82 81 80 79 78 77 76 75 74 73 72 71 70 69 68 67 66 65 64 63 62 61 60 59 58 57 56 55 54 53 52 51 50 49 48

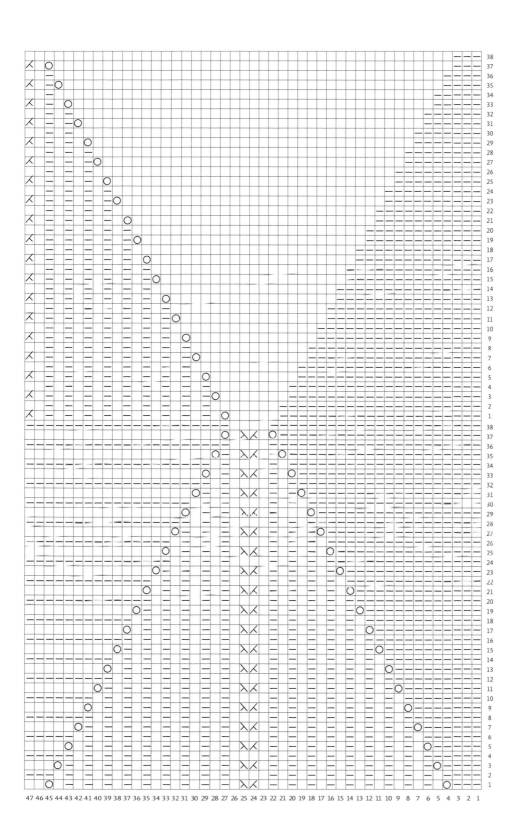

Stitch Key

☐ K on RS, p on WS

⊟ P on RS, K on WS

◩ K2tog on RS

◪ Sl 1, k1, psso on RS

◎ Yo

long night

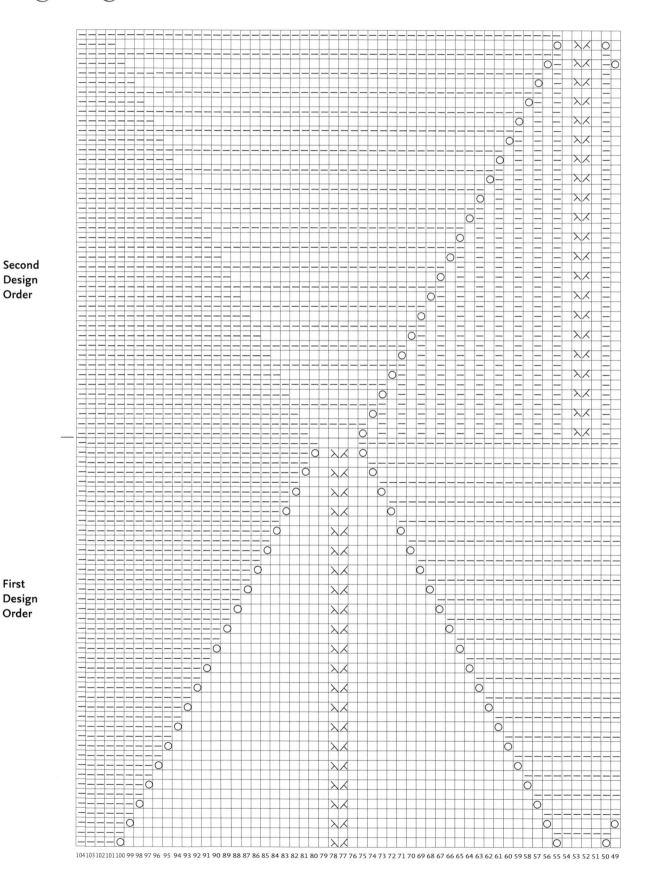

Second Design Order

First Design Order

104 103 102 101 100 99 98 97 96 95 94 93 92 91 90 89 88 87 86 85 84 83 82 81 80 79 78 77 76 75 74 73 72 71 70 69 68 67 66 65 64 63 62 61 60 59 58 57 56 55 54 53 52 51 50 49

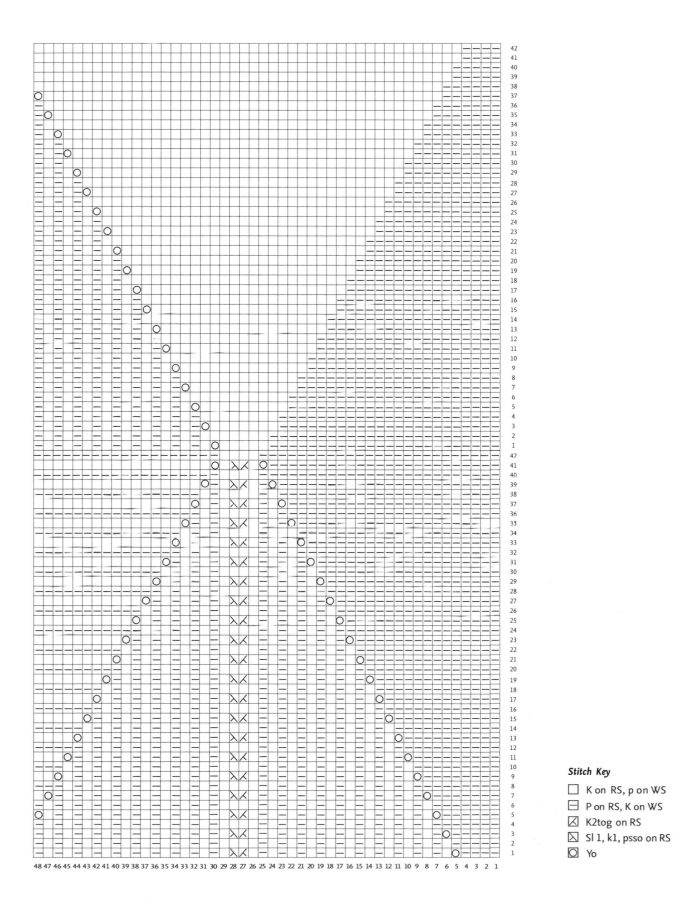

Stitch Key

☐ K on RS, p on WS

⊟ P on RS, K on WS

⧄ K2tog on RS

⧅ Sl 1, k1, psso on RS

◎ Yo

long night

Second Design Order

First Design Order

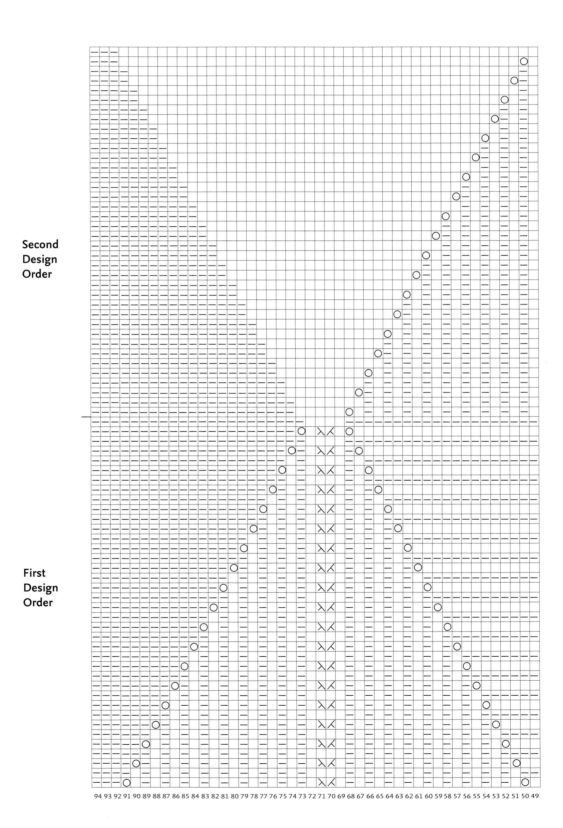

94 93 92 91 90 89 88 87 86 85 84 83 82 81 80 79 78 77 76 75 74 73 72 71 70 69 68 67 66 65 64 63 62 61 60 59 58 57 56 55 54 53 52 51 50 49

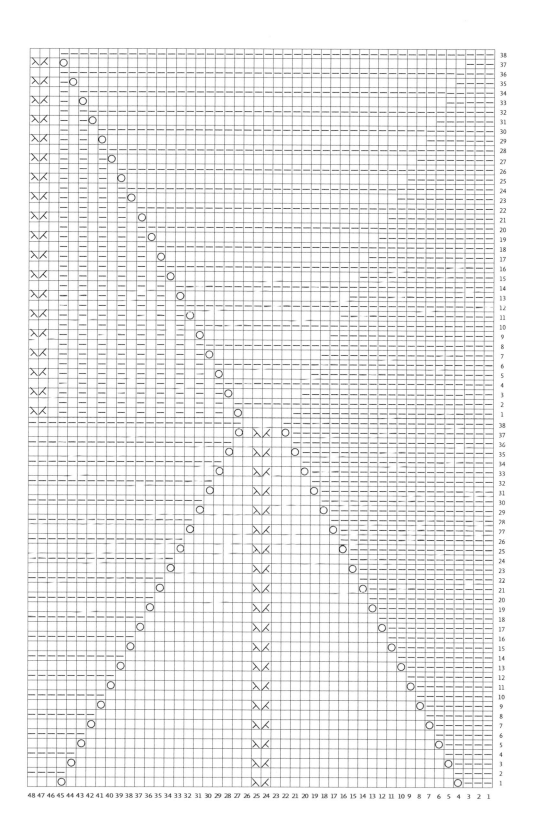

Stitch Key

☐ K on RS, p on WS

⊟ P on RS, K on WS

⊠ K2tog on RS

⊠ Sl 1, k1, psso on RS

◎ Yo

long night

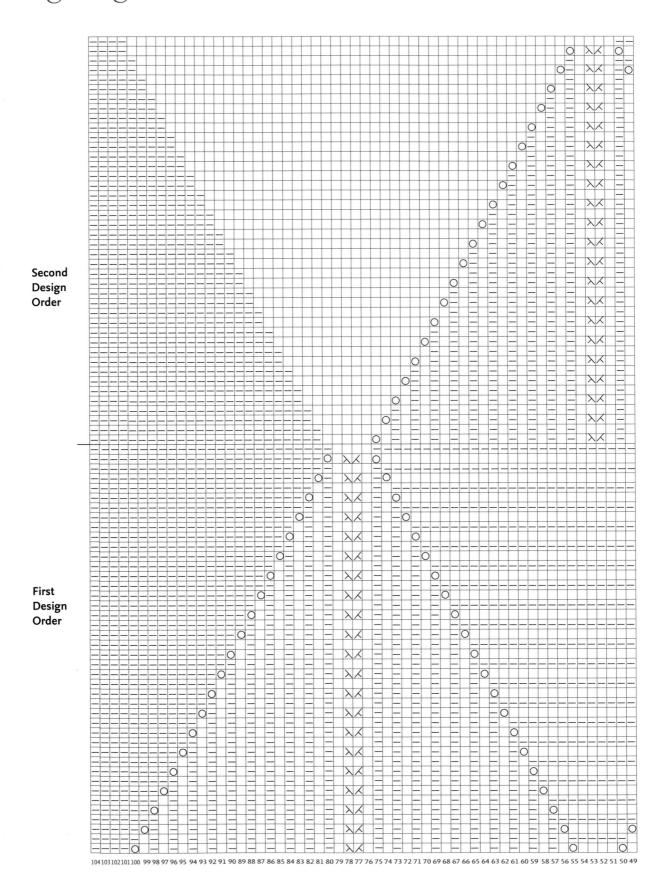

Second Design Order

First Design Order

104 103 102 101 100 99 98 97 96 95 94 93 92 91 90 89 88 87 86 85 84 83 82 81 80 79 78 77 76 75 74 73 72 71 70 69 68 67 66 65 64 63 62 61 60 59 58 57 56 55 54 53 52 51 50 49

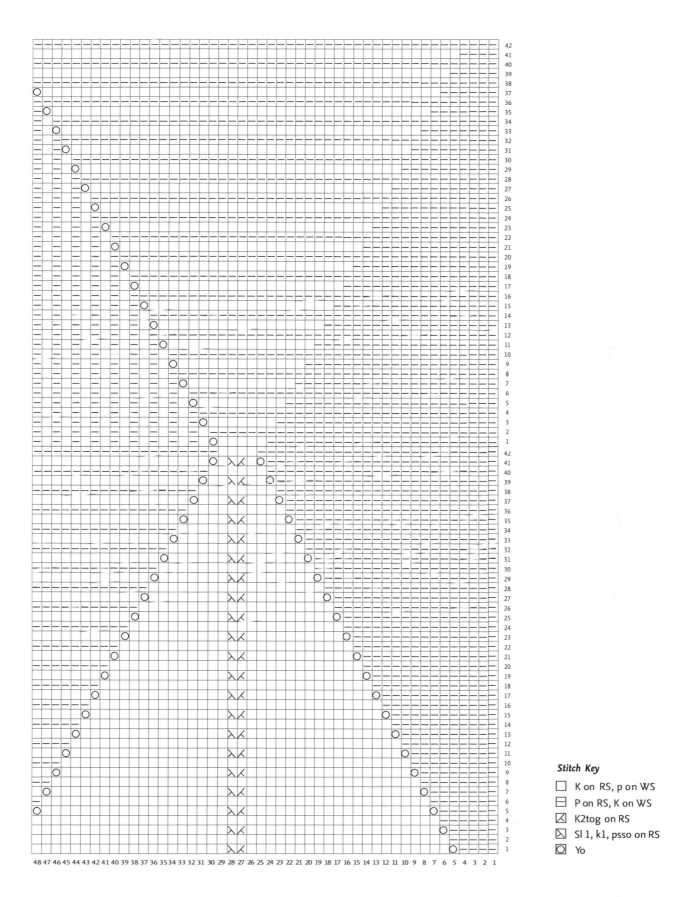

Stitch Key

☐ K on RS, p on WS

⊟ P on RS, K on WS

◺ K2tog on RS

◹ Sl 1, k1, psso on RS

◎ Yo

beauty in motion

Weekend in motion

Express, explore, abandon

Design, determine, dream

windswept grass *flared jumper*

This loosely knit jumper with a slightly flared bottom is shaped without decreases by using various rib patterns for a body-conforming fit. The traveling narrow rib pattern, which starts in a different place on each row creating a diagonal line along its lower edge, is balanced by the wider rib on the upper body, and is offset with a small pocket on the bottom left. The garment is made with two yarns; a cotton-linen blend adds texture to the soft wool-cashmere yarn.

MATERIALS

- RYC Cashsoft Aran (4/medium weight; 57% extra-fine merino wool, 33% micro-fiber, 10% cashmere; 1¾ oz/50g, 95 yds/87m): 5 (5, 6) balls of Oat #1 (A)
- Habu Textiles A-144 (1/super fine weight; 35% cotton, 15% linen, 30% nylon, 20% polyester; 1 oz/28g, 466 yds/426m): 2 cones of Grey #2 (B)
- One each of sizes 10 and 11 (6mm and 8mm) 24" long circular needles. *Adjust needle size if necessary to obtain the correct gauge.*
- Stitch holders
- Stitch markers
- Tapestry needle

GAUGE

14 sts and 18 rows = 4" in St st on larger needles
To save time, take time to check gauge.

STITCH PATTERNS

Stockinette Stitch (St st)
Row 1 (RS): Knit across.
Row 2 (WS): Purl across.
Repeat Rows 1 and 2.

3 x 3 Rib Stitch
Row 1 (RS): K3, p3; repeat across.
Row 2 (WS): Knit the knit sts, purl the purl sts.

1 x 1 Rib Stitch
Row 1: *K1, p1; repeat from * to end of row.
Repeat Row 1.

BACK

With both strands of yarn held together and larger needles, CO 63 (69, 72) sts.

SKILL LEVEL

Easy

SIZES

Small (Medium, Large).
Instructions are for smallest size, with changes for other size noted in parentheses as necessary.

FINISHED MEASUREMENTS

Bust: 34 (38, 42)"
Total length: 24 (25, 26½)"

Work in St st for 4". (If you would like this top to be longer you may increase the length at this time).

Note: As you work the first row you will be changing 3 sts to 1 x 1 rib. Every RS row you will add an additional 3 sts to 1 x 1 rib until all the St stitches have been changed to the rib pattern.

Row 1 (RS): P1, k1, p1, k to end.

Row 2 (WS): P to last 3 sts, k1, p1, k1.

Row 3 (RS): P1, k1, p1, k1, p1, k1, p1, k to end.

Row 4 (WS): P to last 7 sts, k1, p1, k1, p1, k1, p1, k1.

Continue in this manner until all sts changed to 1 x 1 rib.

Work in 1 x 1 rib until piece measures 11 (11½, 12)" from CO edge.

Change to 3 x 3 rib and work for 2 (2½, 3)".

Underarm Shaping

Continue in 3 x 3 rib and BO 6 sts at beg of next 2 rows. Dec 1 st at each edge 2 times. 47 (53, 56) sts.

Work in 3 x 3 rib until back measures 18 (19, 20)".

Begin Neck Shaping

Work 17 (20, 21) sts in 3 x 3 rib and place them on holder, BO 12 (13, 14) sts, work rem 18 (20, 21) sts for left back

decreasing 1 st at neck edge once. Continue in 3 x 3 rib until piece measures 24 (25, 26½)" from CO edge. BO 17 (19, 20) sts.

Attach yarn to 17 (20, 21) sts on holder and work these right back stitches the same as for left back reversing all shaping. (Dec 1 st at neck edge for M and L size only.)

Pocket Lining

Using yarn A only and larger needles CO 14 sts and work 2½" in St st. Place sts on st holder.

FRONT

With both strands of yarn held together and larger needles CO 63 (69, 72) sts.

Work as for back until piece measures 5".

Pocket Placing

(RS) Work in patt to last 24 sts. Place next 14 sts on st holder and work 14 pocket lining sts instead. Knit rem 10 sts.

Continue working as for back including underarm shaping until piece measures 15 (16, 17)".

Neck Shaping

(RS) Work 17 (20, 21) sts in 3 x 3 rib, place these sts on st holder, BO foll 12 (13, 14) sts, work foll 18 (20, 21) sts for right front decreasing 1 st at neck edge once. Continue in 3 x 3 rib until piece measures 24 (25, 26½)" from the CO edge. BO rem sts.

Attach both yarns to 17 (20, 21) sts on st holder and work the left front stitches reversing all shaping. (Dec 1 st at the neck edge for M and L size only.)

Pocket Finishing

Place the 14 pocket sts from the st holder on the front of the garment onto smaller needle. Attach Yarn A and work in 1 x 1 rib for 1½". BO.

FINISHING

Block pieces lightly. Sew front and back side and shoulder seams together with mattress stitch. With 1 strand of Yarn A threaded onto a tapestry needle, whip stitch around the neck and underarm openings. (Crab stitch and Single crochet are optional finishes.) With Yarn A on a tapestry needle secure the pocket lining to the inside front.

windswept grass

flared jumper

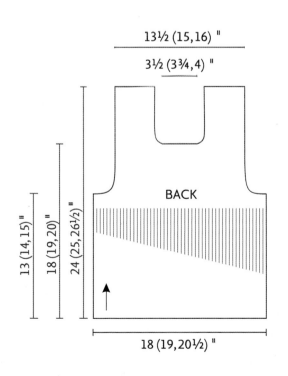

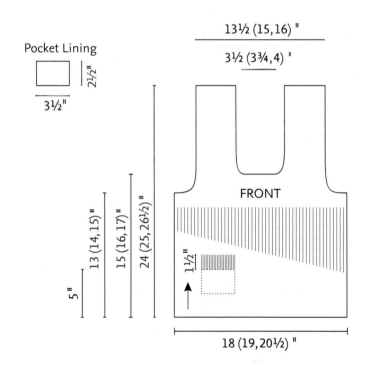

↑ = Direction of work

running brook *racerback tunic dress*

This is a perfect summer tunic dress *for the young at heart. The close fitting A-line style is worked in reverse stocki-nette stitch. The entire dress is knitted from side to side in one piece, and short row shaping adds flare to the bottom edge. A mix of two different yarns, a cotton-viscose-silk blend and a linen yarn, adds texture and depth.*

MATERIALS
- Debbie Bliss Cathay (3/lightweight; 50% cotton, 35% viscose, 15% silk; 1¾ oz/50g, 109 yds/99m): 8 (9, 10) balls of Teal #7 (A)
- Habu Textiles A-60 Linen Paper (4/medium weight; 100% linen; 1 oz/28g, 280 yds/250m): 3 cones of Khaki #117 (B)
- Size 10 (6mm) straight and size 10½ (6.5mm) 24" long circular needles. *Adjust needle size if necessary to obtain the correct gauge.*
- Stitch holder
- Row counter
- Tapestry needle

GAUGE
13 sts and 21 rows = 4" in rev St st with Yarns A and B held together
To save time, take time to check gauge.

STITCH PATTERNS
Reverse Stockinette Stitch (rev St st)
Row 1 (RS): Purl across.
Row 2 (WS): Knit across.
Repeat Rows 1 and 2.

DRESS
Holding 1 strand each of Yarns A and B together, CO 70 (75, 80) sts. Work in rev St st for 12 (14, 16) rows.
Next row (RS): BO 5 sts, p to end.
Continue in rev St st for 26 (28, 30) rows.

First Short Row Shaping
Row 1 (WS): K39 (42, 45) sts, turn
Row 2 (RS): Sl 1, p38 (41, 44).
Row 3: K38 (41, 44), wrap1, turn.

SKILL LEVEL
Intermediate

SIZES
Small (Medium, Large).
Instructions are for smallest size, with changes for other size noted in parentheses as necessary.

FINISHED MEASUREMENTS
Bust: 34 (38, 42)"
Total length: 21½ (23½, 25)" at center back, not including the straps

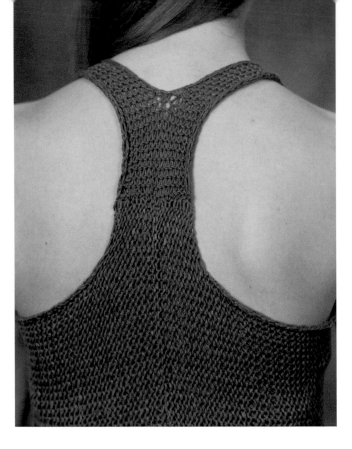

Row 4: Sl 1, p37 (40, 43).

Row 5: K37 (40, 43), wrap1, turn.

Row 6: Sl 1, p36 (39, 42).

Continue in this manner for 5 (7, 9) more rows.

Next row (RS): Sl 1, p32 (34, 36).

Next Row (WS): K65 (70, 75), picking up and knitting each wrap together with st.

Work even in rev St st for 28 (30, 32) rows.

Second Short Row Shaping

Row 1 (WS): K29 (32, 35) sts, turn

Row 2 (RS): Sl 1, p28 (31, 34).

Row 3: K28 (31, 34), wrap1, turn.

Row 4: Sl 1, p27 (30, 33).

Row 5: K27 (30, 33), wrap1, turn.

Row 6: Sl 1, p26 (29, 32).

Continue in this manner for another 17 (19, 21) rows.

Next Row (RS): Sl 1, p17 (18, 20).

Next Row (WS): K65 (70, 75), picking up and knitting each wrap together with st.

Continue even in rev St st for 8 (10, 12) rows.

Next Row (RS): BO 4 sts, p to end.

Work 10 more rows.

Third Short Row Shaping

Row 1 (WS): K39 (42, 45) sts, turn

Row 2 (RS): Sl 1, p38 (41, 44).

Row 3: K38 (41, 44), wrap1, turn.

Row 4: Sl 1, p37 (40, 43).

Row 5: K37 (40, 43), wrap1, turn.

Row 6: Sl 1, p36 (39, 42).

Continue in this manner for 5 (7, 9) more rows.

Next Row (RS): Sl 1, p32 (34, 36).

Next Row (WS): K61 (66, 71), picking up and knitting each wrap together with st.

Work even in rev St st for 8 (10, 12) rows.

Next row (WS): CO 4 sts, k65 (70, 75).

Work even in rev St st for 10 (12, 14) rows.

Fourth Short Row Shaping

Row 1 (WS): K29 (32, 35) sts, turn.

Row 2 (RS): Sl 1, p28 (31, 34).

Row 3: K28 (31, 34), wrap1, turn.

Row 4: Sl 1, p27 (30, 33).

Row 5: K27 (30, 33), wrap1, turn.

Row 6: Sl 1, p26 (29, 32).

Continue in this manner for 17 (19, 21) more rows.

Next row (RS): Sl 1, p17 (18, 20).

Next Row (WS): K65 (70, 75) picking up and knitting each
   wrap together with st.
Work even in rev St st for 28 rows.

Fifth Short Row Shaping

Row 1 (WS): K39 (42, 45) sts, turn

Row 2 (RS): Sl 1, p38 (41, 44).

Row 3: K38 (41, 44), wrap1, turn.

Row 4: Sl 1, p37 (40, 43).

Row 5: K37 (40, 43), wrap1, turn.

Row 6: Sl 1, p36 (39, 42).

Continue in this manner for 5 (7, 9) more rows.

Next Row (RS): Sl 1, p32 (34, 36).

Next Row (WS): K65 (70, 75) picking up and knitting each
   wrap together with st.

Work even in rev St st for 26 (28, 30) rows.

Next row (WS): CO 5 sts, k70 (75, 80).

Work in rev St even for 12 (14, 16) rows.
BO all sts loosely.

FINISHING

Use a traditional mattress stitch to sew the center
   back seam.

STRAPS

With RS facing, pick up and knit 16 (18, 20) sts from point
   A to point B at center back. Work in St st for 3". Work 8
   (9, 10) sts and place remaining sts on st holder. Continue working St st for 9½ (10, 11)" for first strap. BO.

Transfer 8 (9, 10) rem sts to your needle, join yarn, and
   work in St st for 9½ (10, 11)" for second strap. BO.

Attach each strap to the front, from point C to D and
   point E to F, as labeled in the schematic. Block lightly.

running brook
racerback tunic dress

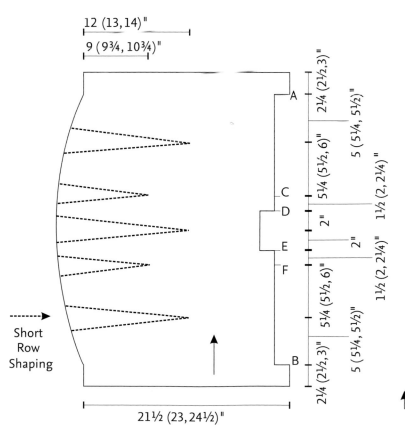

12 (13, 14)"

9 (9¾, 10¾)"

A

2¼ (2½, 3)"

5 (5¼, 5½)"

C

5¼ (5½, 6)"

D

2"

1½ (2, 2¼)"

E

2"

F

5¼ (5½, 6)"

1½ (2, 2¼)"

Short
Row
Shaping

B

5 (5¼, 5½)"

2¼ (2½, 3)"

21½ (23, 24½)"

↑ = Direction of work

bird of passage *raglan swing cardigan*

I've always loved the shape of a bird's wing, but it's difficult to incorporate that distinctive form into an everyday garment without verging on costume. That challenge inspired me to update a traditional raglan sweater by essentially merging it with a wrap, to create an elegant A-line silhouette with fly-away three-quarter sleeves. For the shaping, I used alternating right- and left-slanting decreases, which produce a surface texture that recalls the feather pattern of a bird's wing. The outside raglan seams add an interesting decorative touch. The garment is loose-fitting, which makes it easily adaptable to variety of sizes.

MATERIALS

- Berroco Pure Merino (4/medium weight; 100% extra fine merino; 1¾ oz/50g; 92 yds/84m): 11 (12, 13) balls of Aubergine #8522
- One each of sizes 7 and 9 (4.5 and 5.5mm) 24" long circular needles. *Adjust needle size if necessary to obtain the correct gauge.*
- Five stitch holders
- Stitch markers
- Row counter
- Tapestry needle
- Two ⅝" decorative buttons
- One ½" flat button
- Size B (2.25mm) crochet hook

GAUGE

18 sts and 24 rows = 4" in St st on larger needles
To save time, take time to check gauge.

STITCH PATTERNS

Garter Stitch
Pattern Row: Knit across.
Repeat Patt Row.

Stockinette Stitch (St st)
Row 1 (RS): Knit across.
Row 2 (WS): Purl across.
Repeat Rows 1 and 2.

SKILL LEVEL

Easy

SIZES

Small (Medium, Large).
Instructions are for smallest size, with changes for other size noted in parentheses as necessary.

FINISHED MEASUREMENTS

Bust (buttoned): 32–34 (36–38, 40–42)"
Total length: 18 (19, 20)"

Special Decrease Stitches

Right-Slanting Decrease (RD): Knit 2 sts, place them back onto the left needle, pass the third stitch from left needle over the 2 sts already knit.

Place the 2 knit sts back onto the right needle.

Left-Slanting Decrease (LD): Slip 1 stitch as if to P, knit the following 2 sts, pass the slipped stitch over the 2 knitted stitches.

BACK

With larger needles, CO 102 (106, 112) sts. Knit 9 rows in Garter st. These 9 rows become the bottom band of the cardigan.

Row 1 (WS): Beg St st patt, starting with a purl row. Work a total of 5 rows, ending with a WS row.

Row 6 (Set up Decrease Row) (RS): K9 (9, 10), pm (place marker), RD, k18 (19, 20), pm, RD, k36 (38, 40), LD, pm, k18 (19, 20), LD, pm, k9 (9, 10)

Rows 7-11: Work a total of 5 rows in St st, starting and ending with a purl (WS) row.

Row 12: (Decrease Row) (RS): K9 (9, 10), slip marker (sl m), RD, knit to the next marker, sl m, RD, knit to 3 sts before the next marker, LD, sl m, knit to 3 sts before the next marker, LD, sl m, k9 (9, 10).

Continue in St st working a Decrease row (as row 12) every 6th row 15 (16, 17) more times, and at the same time beginning armhole shaping.

Armhole Shaping

BO 4 sts at the beg of the 6th Decrease Row, and at the beg of the foll row.

Continue with RD and LD on every 6th row until a total of 17 (18, 19) decrease rows are made.

Place rem 25 (27, 28) sts on st holder.

LEFT FRONT

With larger needles CO 63 (67, 70) sts. Knit 9 rows in Garter St. These 9 rows become the bottom left front band.

Row 1 (WS): K12 (13, 14) (front band sts), purl to last st.

Row 2 (RS): Knit across.

Rows 3–5: Repeat rows 1 and 2 ending with WS row.

Row 6 (Set up Decrease Row) (RS): K9 (10, 11), pm, RD, k18 (19, 20), pm, RD, k18 (19, 20), pm, k12 (13, 14).

Row 7 (and every WS row): K12 (13, 14), purl to the end.

Continue Decrease Rows on every 6th row 15 (16, 17) more times as follows: K9 (10, 11) sts, sl m, RD, knit to next marker, sl m, RD, knit to next marker, sl m, k12 (13, 14), and at the same time begin armhole shaping.

Armhole Shaping

BO 4 sts at the beginning of the 6th Decrease Row.

Continue with RD decreases until a total of 17 (18, 19) decrease rows have been completed. Place rem 25 (27, 28) sts on st holder.

RIGHT FRONT

With larger needles CO 63 (67, 70) sts. Knit 9 rows in Garter St. These 9 rows form the bottom right front band.

Row 1 (WS): Purl to last 12 (13, 14) sts, k12 (13, 14) (front band sts).

Row 2 (RS): Knit across.

Rows 3–5: Repeat rows 1 and 2, ending with WS row.

Work rest of Right Front as Left Front except reverse all shaping, and use LD instead of RD.

SLEEVES (make 2)

With larger needles CO 84 (90, 96) sts. Use a row counter in preparation for armhole bind off. Work in Garter sts for 9 rows. These 9 rows become the bottom band.

Rows 1–5: Working St st, begin with a P row and end with a WS row.

Row 6: (Set Up Decrease Row) (RS): K8 (9, 10), pm, RD, k14 (15, 16), pm, RD, k28 (30, 32), LD, pm, k14 (15, 16), LD, pm, k8 (9, 10).

Rows 7–15: Starting and ending with a WS (purl) row, resume St st.

Row 16 (Decrease Row) (WS): K8 (9, 10), sl m, RD, knit to the next marker, sl m, RD, knit to within 3 sts before next marker, LD, sl m, knit to within 3 sts before next marker, LD, sl m, k8 (9, 10).

Work Decrease Rows every 8th row until a total of 13 (14, 15) Decrease Rows are completed. At the beginning of rows 50 and 51, BO 4 sts for underarm. Place rem 24 (26, 28) sts on st holder.

SEAMING

With the wrong sides of a sleeve and the Right Front held together, sew the raglan edges together one stitch in from the finished edge. This will create a decorative seam on the outside of the garment. Continue to seam the other raglan sleeve edges to the Back and Left Front in the same manner.

Sew the two side seams and the two sleeve seams using a regular mattress stitch for a traditional seam on the inside of the garment.

COLLAR

Row 1 (WS): With smaller needles and WS facing you, knit the sts from the st holders in the following order. Begin with the Left Front, then Left Sleeve, Back, Right Sleeve, and Right Front. Knit the last st of each section together with the first st of the next section until all stitch holders have been removed. 119 (129, 136) sts

Row 2 (RS): Cast on 12 more sts onto your left needle.

Rows 3–7: Work in Garter st patt.

Row 8 (Buttonhole Row) (RS): K4, bind off 3 sts, Knit to end.

Row 9 (WS): Knit to 3 bound off sts, CO 3 sts, k4. Continue working in Garter st for 6 more rows.

Rows 16 and 17: Repeat Row 8 (Buttonhole Row) and Row 9.

Rows 18–24: Work in Garter st. BO.

FINISHING

To make a loop for a hidden button that will be sewn on the inside of the right side: With size B (2.25mm) crochet hook, chain 8 sts. Secure this bar to the center of the left front edge of the collar.

Sew the ½" flat button approximately 6" from the right buttonhole edge of collar, placing it in the center of the collar on the wrong side.

Approximately 5" from the left front collar edge sew in place the two ⅝" decorative buttons to match the buttonholes.

bird of passage

raglan swing cardigan

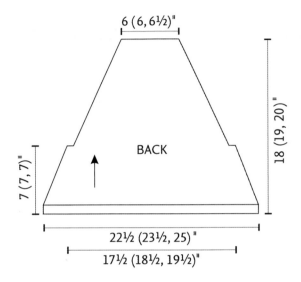

6 (6, 6½)"

BACK

18 (19, 20)"

7 (7, 7)"

22½ (23½, 25)"

17½ (18½, 19½)"

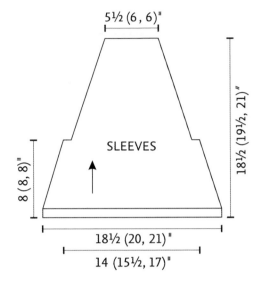

5½ (6, 6)"

SLEEVES

18½ (19½, 21)"

8 (8, 8)"

18½ (20, 21)"

14 (15½, 17)"

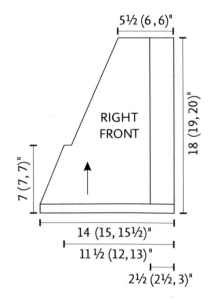

5½ (6, 6)"

RIGHT FRONT

18 (19, 20)"

7 (7, 7)"

14 (15, 15½)"

11½ (12, 13)"

2½ (2½, 3)"

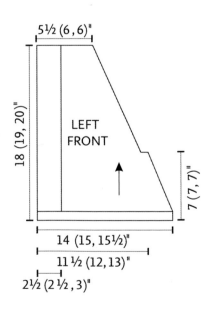

5½ (6, 6)"

LEFT FRONT

18 (19, 20)"

7 (7, 7)"

14 (15, 15½)"

11½ (12, 13)"

2½ (2½, 3)"

↑ = Direction of work

ripened wheat   *linen paper long-sleeve pullover*

I liked playing with yarn textures for this pullover. The linen yarn is especially wonderful; it feels crisp at first and will soften with use. Worked with the silk–stainless steel yarn, the knitted fabric will adjust to your body. This loose-fitting, three-quarter-sleeve pullover, which can be worn as a regular V-neck or off the shoulder, is made in four rectangular pieces and one triangular back insert piece. The combination yoke-and-sleeve piece is knit from side to side.

MATERIALS
- Habu Textiles A-60 Linen Paper (4/medium weight; 100% linen; 1 oz/28g, 280 yds/250m): 3 cones of Green, #114 (A)
- Habu Textiles A-20 Stainless Steel Silk (1/super fine weight; 69% silk, 31% stainless steel; ½ oz/14g, 281 yds/257m): 2 cones of Grey #3 (B)
- One each of sizes 7 and 8 (4.5 mm and 5 mm) 24" long circular needles. *Adjust needle size if necessary to obtain the correct gauge.*
- Stitch markers
- Tapestry needle

GAUGE
16 sts and 20 rows = 4" in St st on smaller needle with Yarns A and B held together. *Gauge is approximate and not crucial for this garment.*

PATTERN NOTE
This garment is knit with Yarns A and B held together throughout.

BODY (make 2, one Front and one Back)
With larger needles CO 90 (94, 98) sts and work 4 rows in St st. Change to smaller needles and work in St st until piece measures 13 (14, 15)" from CO edge. BO loosely.

YOKE AND SLEEVES (make 2)
With larger needles CO 64 (66, 68) sts and work 4 rows in St st. Change to smaller needles and continue in St st until piece measures 9 (10, 11)", place a marker on each edge. Continue working in St st until piece measures 20 (22, 23½)" from the cast on edge. BO loosely.

BACK INSERT
With larger needles CO 2 sts. Work in St st increasing 1 st at beg and end of every RS row until you have 36 (40, 44) sts on your needle. Work 1 more row. BO loosely.

SKILL LEVEL
Easy

SIZES
Small (Medium, Large).
Instructions are for smallest size, with changes for other size noted in parentheses as necessary.

FINISHED MEASUREMENTS
Bust: 44 (46½, 49)"
Total length: 21 (22¼, 23½)"

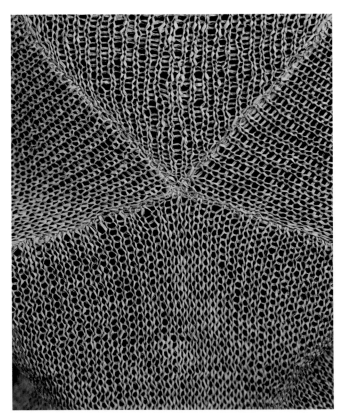

FINISHING

Sew front and back side seams together.

Sew yoke to the body starting from point A (marker) to B
and from point C (marker) to D. Sew sleeves together
from CO edge to the markers. Sew insert to center of
back as shown.

With smaller needles pick up stitches around neck opening and work in St st for 1". BO loosely.

ripened wheat

linen paper long-sleeve pullover

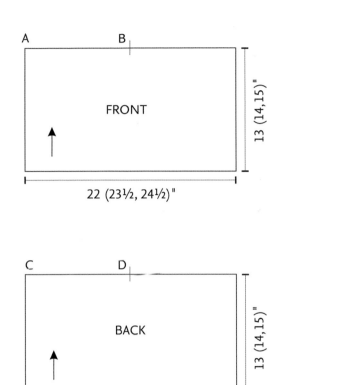

A   B

FRONT

13 (14, 15)"

22 (23½, 24½)"

C   D

BACK

13 (14, 15)"

22 (23½, 24½)"

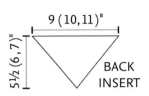

9 (10, 11)"

5½ (6, 7)"

BACK
INSERT

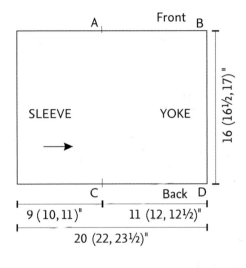

A   Front   B

SLEEVE   YOKE

16 (16½, 17)"

C   Back   D

9 (10, 11)"   11 (12, 12½)"

20 (22, 23½)"

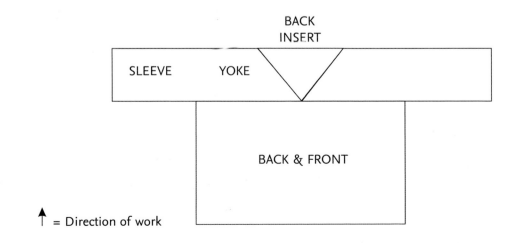

BACK
INSERT

SLEEVE   YOKE

BACK & FRONT

↑ = Direction of work

flickering flame _mohair cardigan with ruffles_

When the dance of a flickering candle was spreading its light around me, I thought of darkness and light, of the dangerous energy of the fire and the softness of the candle flame. These thoughts inspired me to create a cardigan with opposing characteristics; it is austere, but with more than a touch of softness and femininity in its ruffles. The cropped cardigan is knit in a basketweave stitch with silk-mohair and linen yarns held together. The ruffles are worked in Stockinette stitch with one strand of mohair.

MATERIALS

- Habu Textiles A-62 paper moiré (3/lightweight; 50% linen, 50% nylon; 1 oz/28g; 311 yds/284m): 2 (3, 3) balls of Camel #2 (A)
- Habu Textiles A-32 or A-32B mohair silk (1/super fine; 60% mohair, 40% silk; ½ oz/28g; 373 yds/341 m): 2 (3, 3) balls of Gray, #2 (B)
- One each of sizes 9, 10½, and 11 (5.5mm, 6.5mm and 8mm) needles. _Adjust needle size if necessary to obtain the correct gauge._
- Tapestry needle
- Size E (3.5mm) crochet hook

GAUGE

13 sts and 14 rows = 4" on size 11 (8mm) needles with Yarns A and B held together in basketweave stitch

13 sts and 18 rows = 4" on size 10½ (6.5mm) needles with Yarns A and B held together in 1 x 1 rib

18 sts and 20 rows = 4" on size 9 (5.5mm) needles with Yarn B in St st

To save time, take time to check gauge.

STITCH PATTERNS

Stockinette Stitch (St st)

Row 1 (RS): Knit across.

Row 2 (WS): Purl across.

Repeat Rows 1 and 2.

1 x 1 Rib Stitch

Row 1 (RS): K1, p1; repeat across.

Row 2 (WS): P1, k1; repeat across.

Repeat Rows 1 and 2.

SKILL LEVEL

Easy

SIZES

Small (Medium, Large).

Instructions are for smallest size, with changes for other size noted in parentheses as necessary.

FINISHED MEASUREMENTS

Bust: 34 (38, 42)"

Total length: 20½ (21½, 22½)"

Basketweave Stitch (over 10 + 2 sts)

Rows 1, 3, 5 (RS): K1, (k5, p5) across row, k1.

Row 2 (and all even rows): Knit the knit sts and purl the purl sts.

Rows 7, 9, 11: K1, (p5, k5) across row, k1.

Repeat these 12 rows for Basketweave patt.

BACK

With size 10½ (6.5mm) needles and both strands of yarn held together, CO 62 (67, 72) sts. Work in 1 x 1 Rib patt for 5 rows. Switch to larger needles and begin Basketweave patt. Work even until back measures 12 (12½, 13)" from CO edge.

Armhole Shaping

BO 2 (3, 4) sts at the beg of next 4 rows. Dec 1 sts at each side of every RS row 2x, then every other RS row once. 48 (49, 50) sts

Continue working in patt sts until armhole measures 7½ (8, 8½)" from the beg of armhole.

Neck and Shoulder Shaping

Work 17 sts and place them on st holder. BO foll 14 (15, 16) sts and work rem 17 sts.

Next Row (and on the following WS rows): BO 5 shoulder sts twice and at the same time BO 2 sts at the neck edge at the beg of RS row once.

BO rem 5 sts.

Attach yarn and complete other shoulder, reversing all shaping.

RIGHT FRONT

With size 10½ (6.5mm) needles and both strands of yarn held together, CO 34 (39, 44) sts. Work 1 x 1 rib for 5 rows. Switch to larger needles. Work the first 3 sts on the RS and the last 3 sts on the WS in Garter st. Work the remaining sts in the Basketweave pattern. Work even until right front measures 12 (12½, 13)" from CO edge. End with the RS row.

Armhole Shaping

Next Row (WS): BO 3 (4, 5) sts; work to end.

Next Row (RS): Work patt as established.

Next row (WS): BO 2 (3, 4) sts; work to end.

Continue dec 1 sts at armhole edge at the beg of every WS row 1x (2x, 3x), then on every other WS row once. 27 (29, 31) sts

Continue working as established until armhole measures 5½ (6, 6½)". End with WS row.

Neck Shaping

BO 5 (6, 6) sts at the beg of RS row, then BO 4 (4, 5) sts at the beg of foll RS row, then BO 2 (2, 2) sts at the beg of foll RS row. Dec 1 sts every foll RS row 1x (2x, 3x). Work even in patt st until armhole meas 7 (7½, 8)". 15 (15, 15) sts End with RS row.

Shoulder Shaping

BO 5 sts at the beg of every WS row 3x.

LEFT FRONT

Work as for Right Front, reversing all shaping.

SLEEVES (Make 2)

With size 10½ (6.5mm) needles and both strands of yarn
held together, CO 32 (37, 42) sts. Work 1 x 1 Rib for 6
rows. Switch to larger needles and begin Basketweave
patt for 8 rows.

Sleeve Shaping

Inc 1 sts at each edge on 9th row once, every foll 8th row
3x (3x, 4x), every foll 6th row 3x (4x, 3x). Work even in
patt until sleeve meas 17½ (18, 18½)" from CO edge.
46 (53, 58) sts. End with WS row.

Underarm Shaping

BO 4 (5, 6) sts at the beg of next 2 rows. BO 2 (2, 2) sts
each side every other row 5x. BO 3 (4, 4) sts at the beginning of the next two rows. Work 1 row even. 12 (15,
18) sts. BO all sts.

Sleeve Ruffle

With size 9 (5.5mm) needles and Yarn B, pick up and knit
30 (35, 40) sts from CO edge of sleeve.
Next Row (WS) (and every WS row): Purl.
Increase Row (RS): K1, *yo, k1; repeat from * to the end. 59
(69, 79) sts.
Work even in St st for 7 rows, ending with a WS row.
Repeat Increase Row and 7 rows of St st 2 more times.
233 (273, 313) sts.
Attach 1 strand of Yarn A and with both yarns held to-
gether BO all sts.

EYELET BUTTONHOLES

Using your finger, gently create 11 eyelet buttonholes in
your knitted fabric evenly spaced along the Garter st
edge of the Right Front. Using 1 strand of Yarn B and
tapestry needle, secure these openings using a small
whipstitch around the edges.

RIGHT FRONT RUFFLE

With size 9 (5.5mm) needles and Yarn B pick up and knit
80 (84, 88) sts along the Right Front edge from bottom
up. Purl 1 row.
Increase Row (RS): K1, *yo, k1. Repeat from * to end, for a
total of 159 (167, 175) sts.
Work even in St st for 7 rows. Repeat increase row on the
next row (RS). Work even for 9 more rows. 317 (333,
349) sts.
Attach Yarn A, and with both yarns held together BO
all sts.

FINISHING

Using traditional mattress stitch seaming, sew front to
back at shoulders. Sew sleeves into armhole opening
then seam sleeve from ruffle to underarm. Join sides
from bottom to underarm.
With size E (3.5mm) crochet hook and Yarn B crochet in
Crab stitch around the bottom edge beginning with the
Right Front. Continue up the Left Front edge and work
around the neck edge ending at the ruffle.
Attach ½" matching flat buttons of your choice to the
Garter st edge of the Left Front matching eyelet
buttonholes.

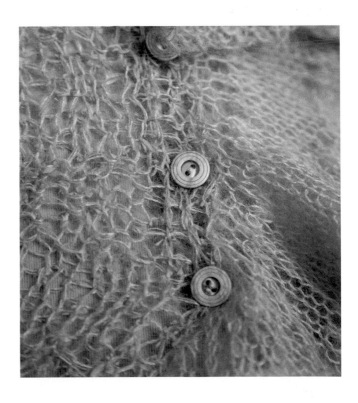

flickering flame

mohair cardigan with ruffles

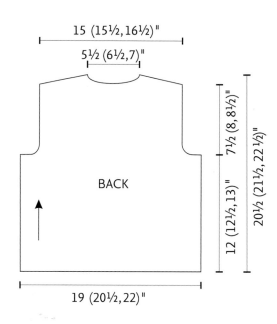

15 (15½, 16½)"

5½ (6½, 7)"

BACK

7½ (8, 8½)"

20½ (21½, 22½)"

12 (12½, 13)"

19 (20½, 22)"

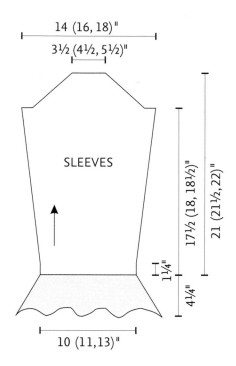

14 (16, 18)"

3½ (4½, 5½)"

SLEEVES

17½ (18, 18½)"

21 (21½, 22)"

1¼"

4¼"

10 (11, 13)"

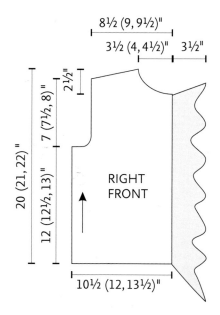

8½ (9, 9½)"

3½ (4, 4½)"   3½"

2½"

7 (7½, 8)"

20 (21, 22)"

12 (12½, 13)"

RIGHT FRONT

10½ (12, 13½)"

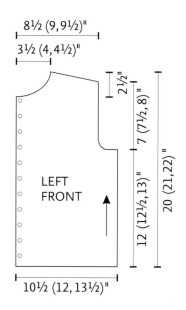

8½ (9, 9½)"

3½ (4, 4½)"

2½"

7 (7½, 8)"

LEFT FRONT

12 (12½, 13)"

20 (21, 22)"

10½ (12, 13½)"

↑ = Direction of work

essential techniques

KNITTING STITCHES

LONG-TAIL CAST ON

Also known as Continental Cast On (CO), this is my favorite cast-on method. It creates a nice, stretchy edge. A guideline for the length of a tail is to leave 1" for every stitch you will be casting on plus 12" extra, but this is a rough estimate only. For fine gauge yarns this may be too much, and for bulky weight yarns you may need to leave more yarn.

1. Make a slip knot on your right needle, leaving a tail of the appropriate length. This slip knot will count as your first stitch.
   Wrap the tail end of your yarn around your left thumb and wrap your working yarn around your left index finger. Secure the ends of the yarn in your palm with your other fingers to keep tension on the yarn.

2. Insert the needle from bottom to top under the loop of tail yarn on your thumb, then from top to bottom over the working yarn held on the left index finger. Draw this strand through the loop of tail yarn to create a stitch on your needle.

3. Remove your thumb from the loop and pull on the tail to secure stitch (do not pull too tight). Continue in this way until the desired number of stitches have been cast on.

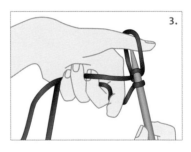

THE KNIT STITCH

The knit stitch (k) is the basis for all other knitting stitches.

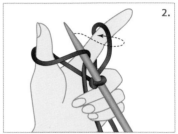

1. Hold the needle with the cast-on stitches in your left hand and the empty needle in your right hand. Keep the working yarn (the yarn from the yarn ball, not the tail) in back. Insert the right needle from front to back through first stitch on the left needle. You will see that the needles form an "X" the right needle beneath the left needle.

2. With your right hand, wrap the yarn counterclockwise under and around the right hand needle.

3. Holding the yarn in place bring the right needle toward you through the center of the cast-on stitch.

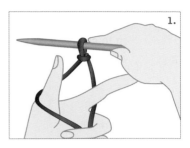

4. Pull the new stitch off the left needle and onto the right hand needle. You have completed 1 new stitch. Repeat steps 1 through 4 until you have completed one row of knit stitches.

THE PURL STITCH

A purl stitch (p) is the opposite of a knit stitch.

1. Holding your working yarn to the front, insert the right needle from back to front through the first stitch on the left needle. Keep the left needle under the right needle. Bring the working yarn over the right needle from top to bottom to create a loop.

2. Pull the loop on the right needle back out through the stitch on the left needle.

3. Slip the stitch off the left needle and onto the right hand needle. This completes 1 purl stitch. Repeat steps 1 through 3 until you have completed as many purl stitches in the row as desired.

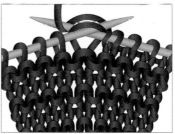

YARN OVER (KNIT)

Yarn over (yo) is a way to create a hole in your knitting for lace or eyelets. Bring the yarn around the right-hand needle from back to front counterclockwise before knitting the next stitch.

Then just knit the next stitch as usual. When you get to the yarn over on the next row, just treat it as a regular stitch and it will form a hole.

YARN OVER (PURL)

Yarn over (yo) is a way to create a hole in your knitting for lace or eyelets. Bring the yarn to the front and over the top of the right needle. Purl the next stitch.

Make sure that when you yo on a purl row your yarn wraps counterclockwise completely around your needle.

On a right side, when you come to the yo, just knit it normally and it will form a hole.

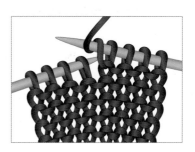

MAKE 1

Make 1 is a practically invisible increase that can be worked purlwise or knit-wise. This increase is made simply by knitting into the horizontal bar between the stitches.

1. Insert the left needle under the strand between the stitch on your right needle and the one on your left needle.

2. Knit into the back of the strand in order to twist the stitch. Slip the strand off the left needle. You now have 1 new stitch (an increase) on the right needle.

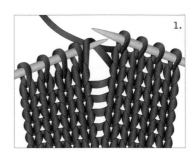

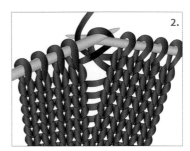

KNIT 1 FRONT AND BACK

Knit 1 Front and Back (k1f&b) is another way to add a stitch.

1. Knit into the front loop as you normally would, but do not slip the stitch from the left needle.

2. Working into the back loop of the same stitch, insert the right needle from front to back through the back loop of the stitch on the right needle. Bring the yarn over and knit through this stitch. Then slip the stitch off of the left needle. There are now 2 stitches worked into the original one stitch.

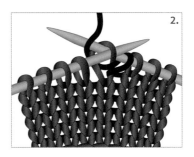

PURL 1 FRONT AND BACK

A variation of this increase is to Purl 1 Front and Back (p1f&b) include purling into the front and back loops.

1. Purl into the front loop as you normally would, but do not slip the stitch from the left needle.

2. Working into the back loop of the same stitch, insert the right needle from back to front through the back loop of the stitch on the right needle. Bring the yarn over and purl through this stitch. Then slip the stitch off of the left needle. There are now 2 stitches worked into the original one stitch.

KNIT 2 TOGETHER

Knit 2 together (k2tog) is the simplest way to decrease. It slants to the right.

1. Insert the right needle into the front 2 stitches on the left needle from front to back and wrap the yarn as if to knit.
2. Pull the loop through the 2 stitches and allow these 2 stitches to slip off the left needle. You have now decreased by 1 stitch.

PURL 2 TOGETHER

Purl 2 together (p2tog), a decrease where you purl 2 stitches together, slants to the right.

1. Insert the right needle into the front 2 stitches on the left needle from back to front and wrap the yarn as if to purl.
2. Pull the loop through the 2 stitches and allow these 2 stitches to slip off the left needle. You have now decreased by 1 stitch.

SLIP, SLIP, KNIT

Slip, slip, knit (SSK) was introduced by Barbara Walker in the 1970s. It creates a decrease that slants to the left.

1. Slip 1 stitch onto the right hand needle without knitting it.
2. Slip the next stitch knitwise. You will have 2 twisted slipped stitches on the right hand needle.
3. Insert the left hand needle through both the slipped stitches from the back. Finally knit the stitches together as if they are 1 knit stitch.

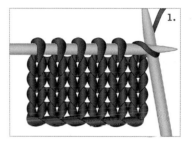

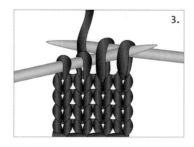

SLIP 1, KNIT 1, PASS SLIPPED STITCH OVER

Slip 1, knit 1, pass slipped stitch over (SKPO) is an older decrease technique than SSK and appears in many lace patterns. SKPO, sometimes abbreviated SKP, slants to the left.

Slip 1 stitch purlwise, that is, insert the right hand needle into the next stitch as if to purl and pass it to the right needle. Knit the next stitch. Insert the tip of the left hand needle into the slipped stitch and lift this stitch over the first stitch on the right hand needle.

SHORT ROWS WITH WRAPPED STITCHES

This technique is used to insert extra rows invisibly in the middle of the knitting to create soft curves or darts in the fabric. They are rows that are only partially worked before turning. You wrap the next stitch before turning a short row to avoid creating holes where you turned the work. When working the row following a wrapped stitch, you hide the wrap by picking it up along with the stitch.

1. To wrap a knit stitch, slip the next stitch purlwise onto the right needle. Bring the yarn to the front of the work.
2. Slip the same stitch back to the left needle.

Turn the work, bring the yarn to the front or back (depending on whether you are knitting or purling), to complete the wrap. Finish working the row.

KNITTING A WRAPPED STITCH

Insert the needle under the wrap from bottom to top, front to back, then knitwise into the stitch itself. Knit the wrap and the stitch together.

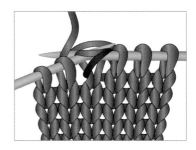

PURLING A WRAPPED STITCH

Insert the needle into the wrap from bottom to top, back to front, then purlwise into the stitch itself. Purl the wrap and the stitch together.

MAKING CABLES

Cables are twists in the knitting where stitches cross over each other. To make a cable, you place a few stitches onto a cable needle (a short, double-pointed needle with a notch or curved section), knit the next few stitches, then knit the stitches from the cable needle. These traveling stitches may move to the right or to the left. To make a left-crossing cable, you hold the cable needle in the front. To make a right-crossing cable, you hold the cable needle in the back.

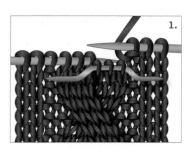

Left Cable

1. Slip the next few stitches onto the cable needle (the pattern will tell you how many; here it's 3) and hold the cable needle in front of the work.
2. Knit the next few stitches from the left needle (again, the pattern will tell you how many; here it's 3).
3. Knit the stitches from the cable needle.

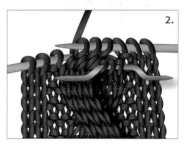

Right Cable

To make a right-crossing cable, you hold the cable needle in back of the work.

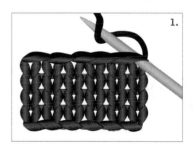

PICK UP AND KNIT

To pick up and knit stitches (PU), you bring a loop of yarn through a hole as if to knit and place it on your needle so that you can knit or purl it later. This hole can be an existing stitch somewhere within the knitted work, at the bound-off edge, or along the side of the work.

To pick up and knit stitches along cast-on/bound-off edge of work

1. By picking up stitches horizontally, you will be extending the structure of the stitches that are already there. This means, you are looking for the V's to identify adjacent stitches. Pick up stitches from the right side (RS) of the work. Holding the yarn to the back, insert your needle through the V of the stitch in the row just below the bound-off or cast-on edge.
2. Wrap the yarn around the needle as if to knit and pull a loop through onto your needle. Continue doing this along the width of the knitting.

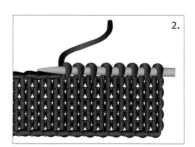

To pick up and knit stitches along side of knitted work

1. With RS of the work facing, insert the needle between 2 purl bars, one stitch from the edge. When working along a straight edge, be sure to pick up stitches in the same line of stitches to create a neat row. When picking up stitches along an edge with decreases, such as a V-neck, be sure to consistently pick up stitches one stitch from the edge to hide the jagged shaped edge.

2. When picking up stitches along the side of knitted work, keep in mind that the row gauge and the stitch gauge are different: A stitch is typically wider than it is high. Because of this, you will skip a row every so often. Unless your pattern specifies a gauge for you to use when picking up stitches along the side, pick up stitches in 3 out of every 4 rows.

MATTRESS STITCH

The Mattress Stitch (also called Vertical Seaming or Row-to-Row Seaming) is an almost invisible seam. It is used to join 2 pieces of stockinette stitch.

1. Start by placing your 2 pieces side by side with the right sides up. Thread the tail (or a new length of yarn) on a yarn needle and insert the needle into the lowest corner stitch on the opposite piece from back to front. Then insert the needle from back to front in the lowest corner stitch on the piece that had the yarn attached. Pull tightly to close the gap.

2. Insert the needle under the bar between the edge stitch and the next stitch in. Pull the yarn through the bar and then insert the needle under the same horizontal bar on the opposite piece. Work back and forth on one piece and then the other. After a few rows, pull the yarn up, not out, to bring the knitted pieces together.

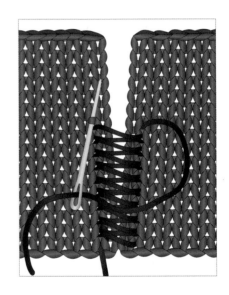

HORIZONTAL SEAM

A horizontal seam joins a bound-off edge to a bound-off edge, and creates the look of another row of knit stitches.

1. Insert the tapestry needle from front, under the V of one stitch, and out to the front of one knitted piece. Insert the tapestry needle into the other piece from the front, under the V of one stitch, and back out to the front.

2. Insert the tapestry needle from the front into the same hole the seaming yarn came out of on the first piece, go under the V of the next stitch, and back out the front. Insert the tapestry needle from the front into the same hole the seaming yarn came out of on the second piece, go under V of the next stitch, and back out the front. Continue this way across the width of the knitting.

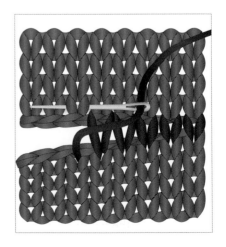

KITCHENER STITCH

The kitchener stitch is a way of grafting live stitches from 2 pieces of knitting so the join looks like another row of knitting.

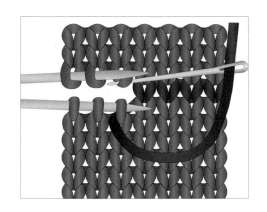

Hold the stitches to be grafted on parallel, double-pointed needles, making sure that the working yarn is coming from the back needle. Insert the tapestry needle through the first stitch on the front needle as if to purl and leave the stitch on the needle. Then insert the needle into the first stitch on the back needle as if to knit and leave this stitch on the needle. Keep the working yarn below the needles. You will now work 2 stitches on the front needle, followed by 2 stitches on the back needle, across the row, as follows:

1. Insert the tapestry needle into the first stitch on the front needle as if to knit, and drop it off the needle. Insert the needle through the second stitch, as if to purl and leave it on the needle. Tighten the yarn.

2. Insert the tapestry needle through the first stitch on the back needle as if to purl, and drop it off the needle. Insert the needle through the second stitch as if to knit, and leave it on the needle. Tighten the yarn.

When there is only 1 stitch on each needle, go through the front stitch as if to knit and drop it off the needle. Go through the back stitch as if to purl and drop it off the needle. Pull the tail to the inside and weave it in.

BASIC BUTTONHOLE

A buttonhole knit over 2 rows is the most basic type. Choose the buttons you want for your project first, making sure the size and thickness of the button will work with your yarn.

1. Knit to the point where the buttonhole will be placed. Bind off the number of stitches needed for the buttonhole. Then complete the row.

2. Knit the next row in pattern. When you come to the point where you bound off the stitches, cast on the same number of stitches, using the Knit Cast On or Cable Cast On. Complete the row.

BINDING OFF

Binding off secures the last row of stitches so they don't unravel. Work loosely when binding off.

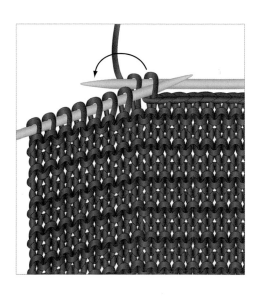

1. Knit the first 2 stitches; insert the left needle into first stitch you knit, and pull it over the second stitch and completely off the needle. One stitch is now bound off.

2. Knit the next stitch, insert left needle into first stitch on right needle, and pull it over the new stitch and completely off the needle. Another stitch is bound off.

Repeat until 1 stitch remains. Cut the yarn, leaving a 6" tail. Slip the last stitch off the needle, draw the tail through the stitch, and pull to close the loop. Thread the yarn end into yarn needle and weave the end into several stitches to secure it.

skill levels

BEGINNER. For first-time knitters. Uses basic knit and purl stitches. Minimal shaping is involved.

EASY. Uses basic stitches, repetitive stitch patterns, and simple color changes. Involves simple shaping and finishing.

INTERMEDIATE. Uses a variety of stitches, such as basic cables and lace, simple intarsia, double-pointed needles, and knitting-in-the-round needle techniques, with mid-level shaping and finishing.

EXPERIENCED. Involves intricate stitch patterns, techniques, and dimension, such as non-repeating patterns, multicolored techniques, fine threads, detailed shaping, and refined finishing.

yarn substitutions

The patterns in this book were each designed with a specific yarn in mind. If you substitute for a recommended yarn, you should choose one with the same weight and a similar fiber content. You should always take the time to make a gauge swatch before you begin a pattern, but it's especially important to do so if you are substituting for the suggested yarn. If necessary, change needle sizes to obtain the correct gauge.

TYPES OF YARN IN CATEGORY		KNIT GAUGE RANGE (in Stockinette stitch to 4 inches)	RECOMMENDED NEEDLE SIZES (U.S./metric sizes)
0 LACE	Fingering, 10-count crochet thread	33–40 sts	000–1/1.5–2.25mm
1 SUPER FINE	Sock, fingering, baby	27–32 sts	1–3/2.25–3.25mm
2 FINE	Sport, baby	23–26 sts	3–5/3.25–3.75mm
3 LIGHT	DK, light worsted	21–24 sts	5–7/3.75–4.5mm
4 MEDIUM	Worsted, afghan, aran	16–20 sts	7–9/4.5–5.5mm
5 BULKY	Chunky, craft, rug	12–15 sts	9–11/5.5–8mm
6 SUPER BULKY	Bulky, roving	6–11 sts	11 and larger/8mm and larger

Adapted from the Standard Yarn Weight System of the Craft Yarn Council of America.

knitting needle conversion chart

U.S. SIZES	METRIC SIZES	U.K./CANADIAN SIZES
0	2 mm	14
1	2.25 mm	13
2	2.75 mm	12
3	3.25 mm	10
4	3.5 mm	-
5	3.75 mm	9
6	4 mm	8
7	4.5 mm	7
8	5 mm	6
9	5.5 mm	5
10	6 mm	4
10½	6.5 mm	3
11	8 mm	0
13	9 mm	00
15	10 mm	000
17	12.75 mm	0000
19	15 mm	00000
35	19 mm	-
50	25 mm	-

knitting abbreviations

* *	repeat steps between asterisks as many times as indicated
beg	beginning
BO	bind off
C	cable
CC	contrast color
cn	cable needle
CO	cast on
DPN	double-pointed needle
foll	following
k	knit
k2tog	knit 2 stitches together (decrease)
kf&b	knit into front and back of same stitch (increase)
LH	left-hand
m1	make 1 stitch (increase)
MC	main color
meas	measures
p	purl
p2tog	purl 2 together (decrease)
pf&b	purl into front and back of same stitch (increase)
pm	place marker
PU	pick up and knit
rev St st	reverse stockinette stitch
RH	right-hand
SKPO	slip 1, knit 1, pass slipped stitch over
sl1	slip 1 stitch
sl 1 kw	slip 1 stitch knitwise
sl 1 pw	slip 1 stitch purlwise
SSK	slip, slip, knit
St st	stockinette stitch
St(s)	stitch(es)
yo	yarn over

metric conversion chart

INCHES TO CENTIMETERS

inches	cm
$\frac{1}{16}$	0.16
$\frac{1}{8}$	0.32
$\frac{3}{16}$	0.48
$\frac{1}{4}$	0.64
$\frac{5}{16}$	0.79
$\frac{3}{8}$	0.95
$\frac{7}{16}$	1.11
$\frac{1}{2}$	1.27
$\frac{9}{16}$	1.43
$\frac{5}{8}$	1.59
$\frac{11}{16}$	1.75
$\frac{3}{4}$	1.91
$\frac{13}{16}$	2.06
$\frac{7}{8}$	2.22
$\frac{15}{16}$	2.38
1	2.54
2	5.08
3	7.65
4	10.16
5	12.70
6	15.24
7	17.78
8	20.32
9	22.66
10	25.40
11	27.94
12	30.48
13	33.02
14	35.56
15	38.10
16	40.64
17	43.18
18	45.72
19	48.26
20	50.80
21	53.34
22	55.88
23	58.42
24	60.96
25	63.50
26	66.04
27	60.58
28	71.12
29	73.66
30	76.20
31	78.74
32	81.28
33	83.82
34	86.36
35	88.9
36	91.44
37	93.98
38	96.52
39	99.06
40	101.60
41	104.14
42	106.68
43	109.22
44	111.76
45	114.30
46	116.84
47	119.38
48	121.92
49	124.46
50	127.00
51	129.54
52	132.08
53	134.62
54	137.16
55	139.70
56	142.24
57	144.78
58	147.32
59	149.86
60	152.40
61	154.94
62	157.48
63	160.02
64	162.56
65	165.10
66	167.64
67	170.18
68	171.72
69	175.25
70	177.80
71	180.34
72	182.88
73	185.42
74	187.96
75	190.50
76	193.04
77	195.58
78	198.12
79	200.66
80	203.20
81	205.74
82	208.28
83	210.82
84	213.26
85	215.90
86	218.44
87	220.98
88	223.52
89	226.05
90	228.60

CENTIMETERS TO INCHES

cm	inches	cm	inches	cm	inches
1	$\frac{3}{8}$	52	$20\frac{1}{2}$	103	$40\frac{1}{2}$
2	$\frac{3}{4}$	53	$20\frac{7}{8}$	104	41
3	$1\frac{1}{8}$	54	$21\frac{1}{4}$	105	$41\frac{3}{8}$
4	$1\frac{5}{8}$	55	$21\frac{5}{8}$	106	$41\frac{3}{4}$
5	2	56	22	107	$42\frac{1}{8}$
6	$2\frac{3}{8}$	57	$22\frac{1}{2}$	108	$42\frac{1}{2}$
7	$2\frac{1}{4}$	58	$22\frac{7}{8}$	109	$42\frac{7}{8}$
8	$3\frac{1}{8}$	59	$23\frac{1}{4}$	110	$43\frac{1}{4}$
9	$3\frac{1}{2}$	60	$23\frac{5}{8}$	111	$43\frac{3}{4}$
10	4	61	24	112	$44\frac{1}{8}$
11	$4\frac{3}{8}$	62	$24\frac{3}{8}$	113	$44\frac{1}{2}$
12	$4\frac{3}{4}$	63	$24\frac{3}{4}$	114	$44\frac{7}{8}$
13	$5\frac{1}{8}$	64	$25\frac{1}{4}$	115	$45\frac{1}{4}$
14	$5\frac{1}{2}$	65	$25\frac{5}{8}$	116	$45\frac{5}{8}$
15	$5\frac{7}{8}$	66	26	117	46
16	$6\frac{1}{4}$	67	$26\frac{3}{8}$	118	$46\frac{1}{2}$
17	$6\frac{3}{4}$	68	$26\frac{3}{4}$	119	$46\frac{7}{8}$
18	$7\frac{1}{8}$	69	$27\frac{1}{8}$	120	$47\frac{1}{4}$
19	$7\frac{1}{2}$	70	$27\frac{1}{2}$	121	$47\frac{5}{8}$
20	$7\frac{7}{8}$	71	28	122	48
21	$8\frac{1}{4}$	72	$28\frac{3}{8}$	123	$48\frac{3}{8}$
22	$8\frac{5}{8}$	73	$28\frac{3}{4}$	124	$48\frac{7}{8}$
23	9	74	$29\frac{1}{8}$	125	$49\frac{1}{4}$
24	$9\frac{1}{2}$	75	$29\frac{1}{2}$	126	$49\frac{5}{8}$
25	$9\frac{7}{8}$	76	$29\frac{7}{8}$	127	50
26	$10\frac{1}{4}$	77	$30\frac{1}{4}$	128	$50\frac{3}{8}$
27	$10\frac{5}{8}$	78	$30\frac{3}{4}$	129	$50\frac{3}{4}$
28	11	79	$31\frac{1}{8}$	130	$51\frac{1}{8}$
29	$11\frac{3}{8}$	80	$31\frac{1}{2}$	131	$51\frac{5}{8}$
30	$11\frac{7}{8}$	81	$31\frac{7}{8}$	132	52
31	$12\frac{1}{4}$	82	$32\frac{1}{4}$	133	$52\frac{3}{8}$
32	$12\frac{5}{8}$	83	$32\frac{5}{8}$	134	$52\frac{3}{4}$
33	13	84	33	135	$53\frac{1}{8}$
34	$13\frac{3}{8}$	85	$33\frac{1}{2}$	136	$53\frac{1}{2}$
35	$13\frac{3}{4}$	86	$33\frac{7}{8}$	137	$58\frac{7}{8}$
36	$14\frac{1}{8}$	87	$34\frac{1}{4}$	138	$54\frac{3}{8}$
37	$14\frac{5}{8}$	88	$34\frac{5}{8}$	139	$54\frac{3}{4}$
38	15	89	35	140	$55\frac{1}{8}$
39	$15\frac{3}{8}$	90	$35\frac{1}{2}$	141	$55\frac{1}{2}$
40	$15\frac{3}{4}$	91	$35\frac{7}{8}$	142	$55\frac{7}{8}$
41	$16\frac{1}{8}$	92	$36\frac{1}{4}$	143	$56\frac{1}{2}$
42	$16\frac{1}{2}$	93	$36\frac{5}{8}$	144	$56\frac{3}{4}$
43	$16\frac{7}{8}$	94	37	145	57
44	$17\frac{1}{4}$	95	$37\frac{3}{8}$	146	$57\frac{1}{2}$
45	$17\frac{3}{4}$	96	$37\frac{3}{4}$	147	$57\frac{7}{8}$
46	$18\frac{1}{8}$	97	$38\frac{1}{4}$	148	$58\frac{1}{4}$
47	$18\frac{1}{2}$	98	$38\frac{5}{8}$	149	$58\frac{5}{8}$
48	$18\frac{7}{8}$	99	39	150	59
49	$19\frac{1}{4}$	100	$39\frac{3}{8}$	151	$59\frac{1}{2}$
50	$19\frac{5}{8}$	101	$39\frac{3}{4}$	152	$59\frac{7}{8}$
51	20	102	$40\frac{1}{8}$	153	$60\frac{1}{4}$

resources

YARN COMPANIES
Berroco: www.berroco.com
Blue Heron Yarns: www.blueheronyarns.com
Cascade Yarns: www.cascadeyarns.com
Debbie Bliss: www.debbieblissonline.com
Eisaku Noro Ltd.: www.noroyarns.com
Habu Textiles: www.habutextiles.com
Knitting Fever: www.knittingfever.com/c/sublime/yarn/
Louet Sales: www.louet.com
Rowan Yarn: www.knitrowan.com
Skacel: www.skacelknitting.com

BOOKS
A Second Treasury of Knitting Patterns by Barbara Walker (Schoolhouse Press, 1998)
Exquisite Little Knits by Iris Schreier and Laurie J. Kimmelstiel (Lark Books, 2004)
Knit Kimono: 18 Designs with Simple Shapes by Vicki Square (Interweave Press, 2007)

WEBSITES
Knitting by the Beach: www.knittingbythebeach.com
Knitting Help: www.knittinghelp.com
Ravelry: www.ravelry.com
Vogue Knitting: www.vogueknitting.com

ORGANIZATIONS
Craft Yarn Council of America: www.yarnstandards.com
The Knitter's Guild of America (TKGA): www.tkga.org

Tanya Alpert *is a knitwear designer, knitting instructor, fiber artist, and the owner of Knitting by the Beach, a yarn store in Solana Beach, California. This is her first book.*

index